Sadi's Bustan And Gulistan

Charles F. Horne

SADI

THE BUSTAN
THE GULISTAN

"In the name of Him who taught the soul to think,
And kindled the heart's lamp with the light of soul."
— SHABISTARI.

SADI

(INTRODUCTION)

SADI was named by a brother poet the "nightingale of the groves of Shiraz." The metaphor might seem to Western taste somewhat too light, when we remember the high repute in which Sadi was held by his nation as a philosopher. To his countrymen, however, he is still chiefly "the nightingale." His foremost place among Persian writers has been explained in the general introduction. He was also noted in his lifetime as a religious teacher, though he never claimed, like his contemporary Jalal, to be inspired by any higher wisdom than that of the human intellect. His religious repute was in part due to his being descended from the race of Mohammed, though his honored family rank did not prevent him from being very poor. He owed his education to charity. Indeed, the very name by which he is now known is but a poetic *nom de plume* assumed to do honor to the prince who aided him in his youth. This charitable ruler was named Sa'd, so the poet called himself Sadi, or "One belonging to Sa'd."

Sadi was not originally a writer. He first devoted a long life to earnest religious exercises, to wide travel, and to study. He is even said to have dipped into the Latin learning of the West, and has been suspected of owing something of his poetic wit to the Latin poet Horace. At all events it was not until Sadi was about seventy years old that, in the year 1256, he settled down in his native city of Shiraz in Southern Persia and there began to write in books the impressions and the wisdom garnered all his life.

The first work of this ripe and remarkable old age was the "Bustan," which means the fruit-garden, or orchard. The book contains, in a rather casual and typically Eastern form, the "fruits" of the author's long experience, his judgments upon life, illustrated by a vast store of anecdotes. These fruits of wisdom Sadi presented in some thousands of poetic couplets, distributed in ten chapters, on such subjects as Contentment, Government, Prayer, and Love.

Scarce two years later followed the "Gulistan," or Rose-Garden, which is usually regarded as the writer's greatest work. It much resembles the "Bustan," except that in this second culling of the opinions gathered through his life Sadi has fallen back on prose, with only occasionally interspersed verse. Nevertheless, if we may judge from the title, Sadi intended this work to be the fairer and lighter of the two, a wandering amid rose-vines rather than under sturdy trees. And its tone is certainly more joyous than that of the "Bustan."

Several other writings, though none quite of equal fame, followed these two. The poet's age was long, and as peaceful as his earlier life had been active. He is said to have lived to be over a hundred and seven years old; but since Eastern legends have woven themselves around Sadi almost as much as around Jalal, we must accept their tales only in a poetic sense. Mysticism has spread its own cloud garment over the great Persian mystic.

There is a typical legend of Sadi's travels for which the reader may care to pause. It is told by an old Persian writer, who says: "Sadi, when in Armenia, became much attached to a young man of his own age. In that country people died not the natural death, but on a particular day, once a year, they were in the habit of meeting on a plain near their principal cities, when they occupied themselves in recreation and amusement, in the midst of which individuals of every age and rank would suddenly stop, make a reverence to the west, gird up their loins, and setting out full speed toward that quarter of the desert, were no more seen or heard of.

"Sadi had often remarked that the relations of those persons made few observations or explanations on their disappearance. At last, on such an anniversary, Sadi observed that his friend was preparing to set off, when he seized upon his girdle, and insisted upon knowing what it meant. The

SADI, THE PHILOSOPHER POET.

From an old contemporary portrait found in Western India where Sadi had travelled.

youth solemnly enjoined him to let him go, for that the Malic-al-mo-at, or angel of death, had already called on him twice, and on the third call he must obey his destiny, whether he would or no; but Sadi kept his hold, and found himself carried along with such velocity as deprived him of the power of knowing whither they went. At last they stopped in a verdant plain in the midst of the desert, when the youth stretched himself upon the earth: the turf opened, and he was swallowed up.

"Sadi threw dust over the spot, lamented him in beautiful verse, and set about finding the way back: he had to cross rivers of molten gold, silver, and copper, through deserts and wildernesses, and over mountains of snow, before he found himself once more at the place whence he had started."

SADI

THE BUSTAN

INTRODUCTION

IN THE NAME OF GOD, THE MERCIFUL, THE COMPASSIONATE!

In the name of the Lord life-creating!
The Wise One speech-creating within the tongue!

The Lord, the giver, hand-seizing!
Merciful, sin-forgiving, excuse-accepting!

A King [1] such that whosoever turned away his head from His door
Found not any respect at the doors to which he went,

The heads of kings, neck-exalting,
Are at His court, on the ground of supplication.

He does not instantly seize the froward;
He does not drive away with violence those excuse-bringing.

And though He becomes angry at bad conduct,
When thou didst return He canceled the past circumstance in the book of sins.

The two worlds (this and the next) are like a drop in the sea of His knowledge;
He sees a crime, but in mercy covers it with a screen.

If a person seeks a quarrel with his father,
Doubtless the father becomes very angry.

[1] *Azize* signifies a king; it is applied to God.

And if a relation be not satisfied with a relation on account
of bad conduct,
He drives him from before him, like strangers.

And if the clever slave is not of use,
The master holds him not dear,

And if thou art kind to friends,
The friend will fly from thee to the distance of a league.

And if a soldier abandons service,
The king army-leading becomes quit of him.

But the Lord of high and low (God)
Shuts not the door of food on any one, on account of his sin.

The embroidered leather surface of the earth is His common
table;
At this open table, whether enemy (infidel) or friend (the
faithful) — what matter?

And if He had hastened against one tyranny-practising,[2]
Who would have obtained safety from the hand of His
violence?

His nature is free from suspicion of opposition and simil-
itude;
His kingdom independent of the devotion of jinn and
mankind.[3]

The servant of His order every thing and person:
The son of Adam, and fowl, and ant, and fly.

He spreads so wide a tray of liberality,
That the *Simurgh*[4] in the mountains of Kaf (the Caucasus)
enjoys a portion.

[2] The first line may also be rendered:
"And, if he had hastened in the way of tyranny."

[3] The nature of God is free from the evil imputation of similitude, and of being of the same nature, made by those opposed to His commands.

[4] "*Simurgh*" is a rare, fabulous bird. See the "Shah-Nameh."

Grace and liberality diffusing, and work executing;
Because He is the Possessor of Creation and Knower of secrets.

Grandeur and egotism are proper for Him,
Whose kingdom is ancient and nature independent.

He places the crown of fortune on the head of one;
He brings another from a throne to the dust.

This one has the cap of Good-Fortune on his head;
That one the blanket of Misfortune on his body.

He makes a fire, a rose-garden for Ibrahim; [5]
He takes a crowd, from the waters of the Nil,[6] to the fire of Hell.

If that (making the fire a rose-garden) — it is the written order of His beneficence;
And if this (the destruction of Pharaoh in the Nil) — it is the sign-manual of His order.

Behind the screen He sees bad acts:
By His own favor He covers them with a veil.

If with threatening He draws forth the sharp sword of Command,
The Cherubim will remain deaf and dumb.

And if from the tray of Liberality He gives victuals to be carried home,
'Azazil (*i.e.,* Satan) will say, "I may carry away a good portion."

[5] "Khalil," meaning "the friend of God," is one of the titles of Ibrahim. Nimrod threw Ibrahim into the fire; but God made the fire a rose-garden for Ibrahim's sake.

[6] This refers to Pharaoh and his host, who were drowned in the waters of the Nile or of the Red Sea.

At the Court of His grace and greatness
The Great Ones have put greatness out of their heads.

In mercy, near to those who are distressed:
A hearer of the prayer of those supplication-making.

Concerning circumstances not yet come to pass, His knowledge penetrating;
As to secrets unspoken, His grace informed.

By power, the Guardian of high (sky) and low (earth),
The Lord of the Court of the day of reckoning (Judgment-day).

The back of a person is not free from obedience to Him (it must bend);
On His word there is not room for the finger of a person (in slander).

The ancient doer of good, good-approving;
With the reed of Destiny, in the womb, picture-painting.

From the east to the west, the moon and sun
He put into motion; and spread the firmament on the water.

The earth, from distress of earthquake, became stupefied;
On its skirt He drove down a mountain as a nail.[7]

He gives to the seed of man a form like a *parì;*
Who has made a painting on the water?

He places the ruby and the turquoise in the back-bone (middle) of the rock;
The red rose, on the branch of green color.

From the cloud He casts a drop toward the ocean;
From the back-bone of the father He brings the seed into the womb.

[7] The earth is supposed to be stretched out flat, like a carpet, with the hills planted on it, to keep it steady.

From that drop He makes an incomparable pearl;
And from this He makes a form (of man) like the lofty cypress.

The knowledge of a single atom is not hidden from Him,
To whom the evident and the hidden are one.

He prepares the daily food of the snake and the ant;
Although they are without hands and feet, and strength.

By His order He portrayed existence from non-existence;
Who, except He, knows how to make the existing from the non-existing?

Another time He takes away (creation) to the concealment of non-existence,
And thence conveys it to the plain of the place of assembling (the Resurrection).

The people of the world are agreed to His divine origin;
Overpowered in respect to the substance of His essence.

The people discovered not what was beyond His majesty;
The vision discovered not the extent of His power.

The bird of Fancy flies not to the summit of His nature;
The power of the intellect arrives not at the skirt of His description.

In this whirlpool a thousand ships of reason foundered,
In such a way that not a plank was found on the marge.

Many nights I sate lost in this journey of thought of God,
When suddenly terror seized my sleeve, saying, "Get up!"

The knowledge of the King (God) is the encircler of the wide plain of creation;
Thy conjecture becomes not the encircler of Him.

Genius reaches not to the substance of His nature;
Thought reaches not to the profundity of His qualities.

One can attain to the Arab poet, Suhban,[8] in eloquence;
But one can not reach to the substance of God without equal.

Because the immature ones have on this road urged the steed of thought,
At the words "*la ahsa,*" they have wearied of the pace.

One can not gallop a steed in every place,
Places there are where it is proper to cast the shield (yield).

And if a traveler (a pious one) becomes acquainted with the secret of God,[9]
They (the angels) will shut on him the door of returning (to the world).

In this banquet (of the mystery of God) they give a cup (of the wine of the love of God) to that one,
To whom they give a draught of senselessness (that he may not utter the mystery of God).

The wise man fears this sea of blood (the mystery of God),
Out of which no one has taken the bark of his life.

Of this hawk (the Rationalist), the eye is sewn up (blind to the knowledge of God);
Of the other (the holy man), the eyes are open (to the knowledge of God); and feathers (of flight to the world) burned.

No one went to the buried treasure of Karun [10] (mystery of God);
And if he found a way, he found not a way out of it.

[8] Suhban Wail was an Arab orator, who was so eloquent that he would not repeat a word, but express his meaning in different language.

[9] As in the traditions (Arabic): "Who knows God, his tongue is dumb."

[10] Karun was born of the uncle, or sister, of Moses. He was famous for his riches. The wealth of Karun is here emblematic of the knowledge of God.

If thou art a seeker, who over this ground (of the knowledge
of God) dost travel,
First thou shouldst pluck up the foot of the steed of returning;

Shouldst reflect, in the mirror of the mind;
Shouldst acquire purity by degrees.

Possibly the perfume of the love of God makes thee intoxicated;
Makes thee a seeker of the Covenant —" Am I your God?"

With the foot of search thou dost travel to that place (the
mystery of God);
And thence thou dost fly with the wing of the love of God.

Truth tears the curtains of fancy;
There remains not a lofty curtain, save the glory of God.[11]

Again for the steed of reason there is no running;
Astonishment will seize its rein, saying, "Stand!"

In this sea of God only the man-guardian (Mohammed)
went:
That one became lost, who went not behind the inviter
(Mohammed).

[11] The Sara of Irak tells us: "God most High, before the creation of Adam (on him be peace), having created the souls of men, said: 'Am I your God?' The souls answered 'Yes.' Those who said 'Yes' in this world became of the faith of Islam. Those who gave no reply remained as infidels. Some of the Moslems, by reason of the affections of this world, forgot that Covenant; but, in the case of the souls of those who are lovers of God, and solitary save as regards Him — its sound still remains. When the perfume makes thee intoxicated and a seeker of the Covenant —'Am I your God?' then, with the foot of search, thou dost find the path to that stage (am I your God?). God most High says to thee —'O Adorer!' and thou dost reply —'O Lord!' Thence, with the wing of love, thou dost fly and arrive at the side of the Court of God, which is the end of the world. Certainty as to the Unity of God is then acquired, and no veil remains between the Adored (God) and the adorer (man) save the veil of splendor, beyond which there is no passing for the steed of thought."

Those persons who have turned back from this road (of following Mohammed)
Traveled much, and are distressed.

That person who chooses the way opposite to the Prophet
Will never arrive at the stage of his journey.

Oh Sadi! think not that the path of purity
One can travel, except behind the Chosen One (Mohammed).

Generous of dispositions, beautiful of natures!
The Prophet of creatures, the Intercessor of nations!

The Imam [12] of the prophets, the Leader of the road!
The faithful [13] of God, the place of descent of the Angel Jibra'il!

The Intercessor of mortals, the Lord of raising and dispersing (the Judgment-day)!
The Imam of the guides, the Chief of the Court of Assembling (the Resurrection)!

The Speaker, whose Mount Sinai is the celestial sphere;
All lights are the rays of his light.

The orphan (Mohammed) who, the Koran uncompleted,
Washed the library of (effaced) so many religions,

When anger drew forth his sword of terror,
Struck, by a miracle, the waist of the moon in two halves.

When his fame fell in the mouths of the people of the world
An earthquake occurred in the court of Kisri (King Naushiravan).

[12] Imam is one who precedes, or leads, the prophets.

[13] Faithful, because Mohammed concealed not any part of the revelation of God. The angel Jibra'il descended on Mohammed with the Koran.

By the words — *lá-iláha illa-lláh* [14] — he broke into small pieces the idol Lat;
For the honor of religion he took away the reputation of the idol 'Uzza.

He brought not forth the dust of the idols Lat and 'Uzza only;
But made the Old Testament and Gospel obsolete.[15]

One night he sate on the beast Burak; he passed beyond the Heavens:
In majesty and grandeur he exceeded the angels.

So impetuous, he urged his steed into the plain of propinquity to God,
While Jibra'il remained behind him, at the tree of paradise.

The Chief of the sacred house (of the Kaaba) spoke to him,
Saying: "Oh, bearer of the Divine Revelation! move proudly higher.

"When thou didst find me sincere in friendship,
Why didst thou twist the reins from my love?"

Jibra'il said: "The power to move higher was not to me:
I remained here because the power of wing remained not to me.

"If I fly one hair's breadth higher,
The effulgence of splendor will burn my feathers."

On account of sins a person remains not in restraint
Who has such a Lord (Mohammed) as guide.

What acceptable praise may I say to thee?
Oh, Prophet of Mortals! peace be on thee!

14 "There is no god but God!"

15 The revelation of the Old Testament descended on Moses; that of the New Testament, or Anjíl, on Isa, or Jesus.

May the benedictions of angels be on thy soul!
May they be on thy companions and followers!

First Abu-Bakr, the old disciple;
'Umar, grasp on the convolution of the contumacious demon (Satan);

The wise 'Usman, night, alive-keeping;
The fourth 'Ali-Shan, Duldul,[16] riding.

Oh God! by the right of the sons of Fatima,
May I, on the word of faith, conclude my life! [17]

If thou dost reject my claim, or if thou dost accept,
I, and the hand, and the skirt of the offspring of the Prophet are together.

Oh chief happy-footed! what loss occurs
Of thy exalted dignity, at the court of the Living One,

That there are a few beggars of the tribe,
Humble companions, guests, at the House of Safety (paradise)?

God praised and honored thee, O Mohammed!
Jabra'il performed the ground-kiss of thy worth.

The lofty sky, before thy worth, is ashamed,
Thou created, and man yet water and clay.[18]

Thou from the first, the essence of the existence of man;
Whatever else became existent is an offshoot from thee.

16 Duldul was the name of 'Ali's mule.

17 In the traditions (Arabic): "He whose last words are '*lá iláha illa-l-láh!*' will indeed enter paradise."

18 In the traditions (Arabic): "Whatever God created — my soul first." And again (Arabic): "I was Prophet, and Adam between water and clay."

I know not what words I may say to thee,
Who art higher than what I say of thee.

To thee the honor of—"but for thee"[19]—is sufficient grandeur;
Thy praise in the verse of the Koran—"*táhá wa yasín*"—is sufficient.

What praise may the imperfect Sadi make?
Oh Prophet! on thee be benedictions and safety!

In the extremes of the world I wandered much;
With every one I passed my time.

From every corner I found pleasure;
From every harvest I obtained an ear of corn.

Like the pure ones of Shiraz of dust-like (submissive) disposition,
I saw not one.—May mercy be on this pure soil of Shiraz!

The cultivating of friendship of the men of this pure soil
Drew away my heart from Syria and Turkey.

I said to my heart: "From Egypt they bring sugar;
They take it as a present to friends."

From all that garden or the world I was loath
To go empty-handed to my friends.

If my hand be empty of that sugar,
There are words sweeter than sugar—

Not that sugar that men apparently enjoy;
But that which the lords of truth take away on paper (with respect).

May the World-Creator have mercy on thee!
Whatever more I may say is empty talk and wind.

[19] According to the holy saying of God (Arabic): "Oh, Mohammed! hadst thou not been, I would not have created the sky."

THE BUSTAN

CHAPTER I

ON JUSTICE AND ADMINISTRATION OF GOVERNMENT

The beneficences of God are not contained in the imagination;
What service does the tongue of praise offer?

Oh God, do thou — this King (Abu-Bakr, son of Sad), the poor man's friend,
Since the ease of the people is in his protection —

Keep long established over the head of the people;
By the grace of devotion, keep his heart alive (fresh).

Keep his tree of hope fruitful;
His head green, and his face, with mercy, fair.

Oh Sadi! go not in the way of dissimulation (in regard to the King's praise);
If thou hast honesty, bring and come.

Thou (Sadi) art a stage-recognizer, and the King a road-traveler:
Thou art a speaker of truth; and the King the hearer of truths.

What necessity that nine thrones of the sky
Thou dost place below the foot of the King Kizil-Arsalan.

Say not: Place thy foot of honor on the Heavens.
Say: Place the face of sincerity in the dust.

Place, in devotion, the face on the threshold of God;
Because this is the highway of the righteous.

If thou (Abu-Bakr) art a slave of God, place thy head on this door of God;
Place from off thy head the cap of lordship.

At the Court of the Order-giver possessed of Majesty,
Bewail, like a dervish, before a rich and powerful man.

When thou dost perform thy devotions, put not on the kingly raiment;
Like the poor dervish, bring forth a cry,

Saying: "O Omnipotent One! Thou art powerful;
Thou art strong; Thou art the dervish-cherisher.

"I (Abu-Bakr) am neither a monarch nor an order-giver;
I am one of the beggars of this Court.

"What springs forth from the power of my conduct,
Unless the power of Thy grace is my friend?

"Give to me the means of liberality and goodness;
And if not — what goodness can come from me to any one?

"O God! keep me on the work of goodness;
Otherwise, no work can come from me."

At night, like the beggars, pray with ardor,
If, by day, thou dost exercise sovereignty.

The obstinate ones (courtiers) are at thy door, loin-girt;
Thou shouldst be thus — thy head on the threshold of devotion.

Oh, excellent! — for us slaves, the Lord God;
For the lord a slave, duty-performing.

They relate a story of the great men of the faith,
Recognizers of the truth of the essence of truth,

As follows: A pious man sate on a panther;
Snake in hand, he urged his long, pleasant-paced steed.

One said to him: "Oh, man of the way of God!
Guide me to this road by which thou didst go.

"What didst thou, that the rending animal became obedient to thee?
That the seal-ring of good fortune went to thy name?"

He said: "If the panther and snake be submissive to me,
And if also the elephant and vulture — be not astonished.

"Do thou also from the order of the Ruler (God) twist not thy neck,
So that no one, from thy order, may twist his neck."

When the ruler is obedient to God,
God is his Protector and Friend.

It is impossible when He loves thee
That He will leave thee in the power of an enemy.

This is the road, and turn not thy face from the way;
Place thy foot on this road and obtain the object which thou dost desire.

Advice of a person is profitable to a person — to him,
To whom the saying of Sadi is agreeable.

I have heard that, at the time of the agony of the soul (the last breath),
King Naushiravan the Just thus spoke to Hurmuz, his son,

Saying: "Be observant of the heart of the poor;
Be not in the desire of thy own ease.

"A person rests not within thy territory
When thou dost seek thy own ease and no more.

"In the opinion of the wise it is not approved —
The shepherd asleep, and the wolf among the sheep.

"Go: protect the poor and needy one,
Because the king is the crown-holder for the sake of his subjects.

"The subject is like the root, and the king the tree;
Oh son! the tree is strong by reason of the root.

"So long as thou canst, wound not the heart of the people;
But if thou dost — thou dost pluck up thy own roots.

"If a straight road (of safety) is necessary for thee —
The way of the pious is hope and fear.

"The disposition of man is toward wisdom,
In the hope of goodness, and fear of wickedness."

If thou didst find these two doors (hope and fear) in the King,
Thou didst obtain shelter in the territory of his kingdom.

The King brings a gift to the hopeful one,
In hope of the gift of pardon of the Creator of the World.

"The injury of persons is not pleasing to him (the king),
Who fears lest injury should come to his kingdom.

"And if there is not this disposition in his nature
There is not the perfume of ease in that territory.

"If thou art foot-bound (by wife and family), accept contentment;
But if thou art a single horseman (solitary), take thy own desire.

"Seek not plenteousness in that land and region,
Where thou dost see the subjects of the king sorrowful.

"Fear not the proud, haughty ones;
Fear that one who fears God.

"In a dream, he sees the territory of another populous,
Who keeps the heart of the people of his country distressed.

"From violence come ruin and ill-fame;
The prudent man reaches to the profundity of this speech.

"It is not proper with injustice to slay the peasants,
Who are the shelter and support of the kingdom.

"For thy own sake preserve the villagers;
Because the laborer of happy heart executes more work for his master.

"It is not manliness to do ill to that one (the villager),[1]
From whom thou mayst have experienced much benefit in tribute."

I have heard that King Khosru [2] said to his son Shirwiya
At that time when his eyes slept (rested) from seeing (at the time of death) —

"In that state be, so that whatever resolution thou mayst make
Thou mayst consider the peace of the peasant.

"Be sure, so long as thou dost not turn thy head from equity and judgment,
That men will not turn aside their feet from thy power.

1 The splendid clothes and delicate food of kings, and other delights of life, are purchased with the gold of the villagers.

2 Khosru Parviz, son of Hurmuz, reigned A. D. 590–625. He was the lover of Shireen. Shirwiya, in order to increase his sensual appetite, took a medicine which proved to be poison: he reigned six months.

" The peasant flies from the tyrant;
He makes his bad repute a stock story in the world.

" Much time passes not, that his own foundation,
That one plucked up, who laid a bad foundation (of tyranny).

" The enemy, skilful with the sword, lays waste,
Not so much as the smoke (grief) of the heart of an old
woman.

" The lamp of grief that the widow-woman lighted up —
Thou mayst often have seen that it burned a city.

" Who in the world is more favored than that one
Who with justice, in sovereignty, lived?

" When the time of his traveling from this world arrives,
The people of the world send mercy to his tomb.

" Since bad and good men pass away,
It is best indeed that they connect thy name with goodness
and bless thee.

" Appoint the God-fearing one over the peasant;
Because, the abstinent one is the architect of the country.

" That liver-eater of the people is thy enemy,
Who seeks thy profit, in the injury of the people.

" Government is a fault in the hands of those persons,
From whose power, the hands of the people are uplifted in
prayer before God.

" The cherisher of good sees not evil;
When thou dost cherish evil thou art the enemy of thy own
life.

"Exercise not retribution against the despoiler by confiscation of his property;
But it is proper to bring forth (to destroy) his root from the foundation.

"Exercise not patience with the agent of the friend of tyranny;
Since, on account of his fatness (from extortion), it is proper to flay his skin.

"It is also proper, at first, to cut off the wolf's head,
Not at the time when he tore in pieces the sheep of men."

How well said the captive merchant
When the robbers gathered around him with arrows! —

"Inasmuch as courage comes from highwaymen,
Whether the men of the army, or a troop of women, what matter?"

The great king who injured the merchants
Shut the door of well-being on the people of the city and the army.

How many wise men again go there
When they hear the rumor of bad custom?

Are a good name and favorable reception necessary to thee? —
Hold in esteem merchants and envoys.

Merchants heartily cherish travelers,
Because they carry their good name to the world.

That kingdom soon becomes ruined
From which the injured heart becomes a traveler.

Be the acquaintance of the foreigner, and friend of the traveler,
Because the traveler is one who hawks about a good name.

Hold dear the guest, and precious the traveler;
But also be on guard from injury from them.

To beware of the stranger is good;
Because, possibly, he may be an enemy in the guise of a friend.

Advance the rank of thy own old friends;
Because treachery never comes from the cherished one.

When thy servant becomes old,
Forget not the right of his years.

If old age has bound the hand of his service —
Yet thou hast power, in respect to liberality.

To accomplish the desire of the hopeful
Is better than to break the bonds of a thousand fettered ones.

If the pillar of the office of the scribe
Falls, he cuts not the rope of hope.

The just monarch, with his subjects,
Becomes angry like a father with a son.

Sometimes he strikes him so that he becomes sorrowful;
Sometimes he makes water flow from his pure eyes.

When thou dost exercise gentleness, the enemy becomes bold;
But if thou art an anvil, he becomes wearied of thee.

Severity and mildness together are best,
Like the vein-striker (bleeder), who is surgeon and plaster-placer.

Be generous, and pleasant-tempered, and forgiving;
Even as God scatters favor over thee, do thou scatter over the people.

No one came into the world who remained,
Save that one whose good name remained.

That one died not, after whom there remained —
Bridge, or *masjid,* or *khan,* or guest-house.

Every one behind whom a token remained not —
The tree of his existence brought not forth fruit.

If he departed from this world and the marks of his well-doing remained not,
It is not fit to chaunt after his death —"*Al hamd!*"

When thou dost wish that thy name may be eternal,
Conceal not the good name of the great ones.

After thy own time (death) call to mind that same descriptive picture
That, after the age of former kings, thou didst behold.

One took away a good name from the world;
The bad custom of the other remained behind him forever.

With the ear of approval, listen not to a person's injury;
But if the speech comes, probe its depth.

Accept the excuse of forgetfulness of the sinner;
When he asks for protection, give protection.

If a sinner comes to thy shelter,
It is not proper to slay him at the first fault.

When once they uttered advice, and the sinner heard not;
Punish him, the second time, with imprisonment and bonds.

And if advice and bonds are of no advantage to him,
He is an impure tree; pluck up his roots.

When anger comes to thee, on account of a person's crime,
Reflect much on his punishment;

Because it is easy to break the ruby of Badakhshan.
Broken — it is not possible to fasten it together again.

. . . .

I heard that King Jamshid,[3] of happy nature,
Wrote on a stone, at a fountain-head:

"At this fountain many like us took rest;
They departed in death, just as the eyes twinkled.

"With manliness and force they took the world;
But they took it not with themselves to the tomb.

"They departed, and each one reaped what he sowed:
There remained only good and bad fame."

When thou hast power over an enemy,
Injure him not; because this (the power) is indeed sufficient sorrow to him.

A living enemy, head-revolving (raging) about thee in desire of thy blood,
Is better than his life-blood revolving (circulating) about thy neck.

I heard that Darius, of august family,
Became separated, on a hunting-day, from his retinue;

A herdsman came running toward him:
Darius, of happy sect, said to his heart:

[3] Jamshid was a famous Persian king who practised sorcery, by which jinns and devils became subject to him. It is said he reigned three hundred years, during which time there was no sickness among the people. At length he laid claim to godship, and was slain by Zuhhak.

"Perhaps this is an enemy who has come to battle:
From a distance I will pierce him with a white poplar arrow."

He adjusted the royal bow to the bow-string:
He desired in a moment to make his existence non-existence.

The herdsman said: "Oh, Lord of Iran and Turan! —
May the evil eye be far from thy time! —

"I am he who cherishes the King's horses;
In this meadow I am in thy service."

The heart of the King, which had gone in fear, returned to its place.
He laughed and said: "O one of contemptible judgment!

"The auspicious angel (Jibra'il) assisted thee;
Otherwise, I had brought the bow-string to the ear."

The guardian of the land-pastured laughed and said:
"It is not proper to conceal advice from a benefactor;

"It is not laudable deliberation, nor good judgment,
That the King knows not an enemy from a friend.

"The condition of living in greatness is such
That thou shouldst know each humble person — who he is.

"Thou hast many times seen me in the presence:
Thou hast asked me concerning the herd of horses and the meadow.

"Now in love I returned before thee:
Thou dost not again recognize me from an enemy.

"O renowned monarch! I am powerful;
Because I can bring a particular horse out of a hundred thousand.

"By reason of wisdom and judgment, I have the guardianship of the horses;
Thou also shouldst keep thy own herd permanent (free from loss)."

When Darius heard this counsel from the man
He spoke fairly to him, and did him kindness.

Darius kept going and saying in his shame —
It will be proper to write this advice on the heart.

On account of anarchy there may be sorrow in that throne and country
When the deliberation of the king may be less than that of the shepherd.

How mayst thou hear the lament of one crying for justice —
The curtain of thy bed-place at Saturn?

So sleep that the lamentation may come to thy ear
If the crier for justice brings forth a shout.

Who complains of the tyrant who is in thy time,
When every violence that he commits is thy violence?

The dog tore not the skirt of one of a Karawan,
But the ignorant villager, who cherished the dog.

Oh Sadi! thou camest boldly into speech:
When the sharp sword of true speech is at thy hand, be victorious.

Say what thou dost know; because truth spoken is well:
Thou art not a bribe-taker, nor a blandishment-giver (hypocrite).

Bind avarice to thyself, but then wash the book of philosophy;
Bid farewell to avarice, and say whatever thou dost desire.

A certain neck-exalting one (a king) in Media came to know
That a wretched one beneath an arch kept saying:

"Thou even art hopeful at the door of God:
Then accomplish the hope of those door-sitting."

Thou dost not wish that thy heart may be sorrowful —
Bring forth from fetters the heart of the sorrowing ones.

The distress of the heart of the one justice-seeking
Casts a king from his kingdom.

Thou hast slept cool half a day in the retired place (harem);
Say to the foreigner, burn in the heat outside.

God is the taker of justice for that person
Who can not ask for justice from a king.

One of the great ones, possessed of discretion,
Tells a story of the son[4] of King 'Abdu-l-'Aziz,

Saying: He had a ring-stone set in a ring,
In respect to the value of which the Court jeweler was confounded.

At night, thou wouldst say it is the orb, world-illuminating;
A glittering star it was, in light like the day.

By chance a drought-year occurred,
When the full-moon of the face of men became the new-moon.

When he saw not ease and strength in man,
He considered it not manliness to be himself at ease.

When a person sees poison in the jaws of men,
How will the sweet water pass to his throat?

[4] The name of the son was Omar, a just and liberal prince.

He ordered: they sold the ring-stone for silver
Because pity came to him, on account of the poor and orphan.

He gave its value, in spoil, in one week:
He gave to the poor, and needy, and necessitous.

Those reproach-making fell on him,
Saying: " Such a ring will not again come to thy hand."

I heard that he said, and the rain of tears
Ran down, like wax, on his cheeks —

As follows: " Ugly is the ornament on a monarch,
The heart of a citizen afflicted with powerlessness;

" A ring without a stone is fit for me:
The heart of a sorrowful populace is not fit for me."

If a relation of the enemy be friendly to thee,
Beware; be not secure of craftiness.

Because his heart becomes torn for vengeance against thee.
When memory of the love of his own relation comes to him.

Consider not the sweet words of an enemy;
For it is possible there is poison in the honey.

That one took his life safe from the trouble of the enemy
Who reckoned friends as enemies.

That knave preserves the pearl in his purse,
Who considers all people purse-cuts.

The soldier who is an offender against the Amir,
So long as thou canst — take not into service.

He knew not gratitude toward his own chief;
He knows not thee also: be afraid of his deceit.

Hold (consider) him not strong as to oath and covenant;
Appoint a secret watchman over him.

Make long the tether of the aspirant;
Break it not, lest thou shouldst not see him again.

When, in battle and siege, the enemy's country
Thou seizest — consign it to the prisoners.

Because when a captive plunges his teeth in blood,
He drinks blood from the tyrant's throat.

When thou pluckest away a territory from the enemy's clutch,
Keep the peasantry in more order than he.

For, if he beats open the door of conflict,
The people will pluck out the essence of his brain.

But if thou causest injury to the citizens,
Shut not vainly the city-gate in the enemy's face.

Say not: "The enemy, sword-striking, is at the gate!"
When the enemy's partner is within the city.

Essay with deliberation battle with the enemy;
Reflect on counsel; and conceal thy resolution.

Reveal not the secret to every one;
For I have seen many a cup-sharer a spy.

Sikander, who waged war with the Easterns,
Kept, they say, his tent-door toward the west.

When Bahman wished to go to Zawulistan,
He cast a rumor of his going to the left, and went to the right.

If one, besides thee, knows what thy resolve is —
It is fit to weep over that judgment, and knowledge, and resolution.

Exercise liberality — neither conflict nor rancor —
That thou mayst bring a world beneath thy signet-ring.

When a work prospers through courtesy and pleasantness,
What need of severity and arrogance?

Thou wishest not that thy heart should be sorrowful?
Bring forth from bondage the hearts of those sorrowful.

The army is not powerful by the arm;
Go; ask a blessing from the feeble.

The prayer of the hopeful weak ones
Is of more avail than the manly arm.

Whosoever takes to the dervish his request for aid,
If he strikes at Firidun, he would overcome him.

Chapter II

ON BENEFICENCE

If thou art wise, incline to truth;
For truth, not the semblance, remains in its place.

To whomsoever there was neither knowledge nor liberality nor
piety —
In his form there was no reality.

Beneath the clay sleeps at ease that one
By whom men sleep tranquil at heart.

Suffer thy own grief in life; for the relation,
Through his own avarice, busies not himself with one dead.

Give now gold and silver which is thine;
For after thy death it is out of thy command.

Thou wishest not that thou shouldst be distressed in heart?
Put not out of thy heart those distressed.

Scatter treasures in alms to-day, without delay;
For to-morrow the key is not in thy hand.

Take away with thy self thy own road-provisions;
For compassion after death comes from neither son nor wife.

That one takes away the ball of empire from this world
Who took, with himself, a portion to the future world.

With sympathy, like my finger-tip,
No one in the world scratches my back.

Place now, on the palm of the hand, whatever there is;
Lest that, to-morrow (the Judgment-day), thou shouldst with the teeth bite the back of the hand.

Strive as to covering the shame of the dervish,
That the veil of God may be thy secret (defect) -concealer.

Turn not the foreigner portionless from thy door,
Lest that thou shouldst become a wanderer in beggary at doors.

The great one causes alms to reach the indigent;
For he fears that he may become necessitous (as to the need of others).

Look into the state of the heart of those wearied;
For thy heart may, perhaps, one day be broken.

Make the hearts of those dejected happy;
Remember the day of helplessness (the Judgment-day).

Thou art not a beggar at the doors of others;
Drive not, in thanks to God, a beggar from thy door.

Cast protection over the head of the one father-dead;
Scatter his dust of affliction, and pluck out his thorn.

Knowest thou not how very dejected his state was?
May a rootless tree be ever green? [1]

When thou seest an orphan, head lowered in front from grief,
Give not a kiss to the face of thy own son.

If the orphan weeps, who buys for his consolation?
And if he becomes angry, who leads him back to quietude?

[1] The father is the root; the son, the branches of the tree. A tree's freshness is due to its root.

Beware! that he weep not; for the great throne of God
Keeps trembling when the orphan weeps.

Pluck out with kindness the tear from his pure eye;
Scatter with compassion the dust of affliction from his face.

If his (the father's) protection departed from over his head,
Do thou cherish him with thy own protection.

I esteemed my head crown-worthy at that time
When I held my head in my father's bosom.

If a fly had sate on my body,
The heart of some would have become distressed.

If now enemies should bear me away captive,
None of my friends is a helper.

For me is acquaintance with the sorrows of orphans,
For in childhood my father departed (in death) from my head.

A certain one plucked out a thorn from an orphan's foot;
The Khujand Chief saw him in a dream:

He was talking and sauntering in the gardens of Paradise,
Saying: "How many roses blossomed from that thorn!"

So long as thou canst, be not free from mercy;
For they bear pity to thee, when thou bearest pity.

When thou hast done a favor, be not self-worshiping,
Saying: "I am a superior, and that other an inferior."

Say not: "The sword of Time has cast him!"
For the sword of Time is yet drawn.

When thou seest a thousand persons prayer-uttering for the empire,
Give thanks to God for favors.

For the reascn that many men have expectation from thee,
Thou hast expectation at the hand of none.

I have said that liberality is the character of chiefs;
I uttered a mistake — it is the quality of prophets!

I have heard that, one week, a son of the road (a traveler)
Came not to the guest-house of Ibrahim, the friend of God.

Through his happy disposition, he used not to eat in the morning,
Unless one, foodless, came from the path of travel.

He went out, and looked in every direction;
Glanced in the quarters of the valley; and saw:

One, willow-like, in solitude, in the desert;
His head and hair white with the snow of old age.

For consolation he said to him: "Marhaba!"
Uttered, according to the custom of the liberal, the invitation,

Saying: "Oh pupil of my eyes!
Do me a favor, as to bread and salt."

He said, "Yes"; and sprang up and lifted his feet;
For he knew his temperament — on him be peace!

The guards of the guest-house of Ibrahim
Placed the abject old man, with respect.

He ordered; and they arranged the table;
All sate around.

When the company began: "*Bismi-llah!*"
A word from the old man reached not his ear.

He spoke to him, thus: "O old man of ancient days!
I behold not thy truth and heart-burning, like old men.

"When thou eatest food, is it not the custom
That thou shouldst take the name of the Lord of Victuals?"

He said: "I accept not a religion
Which I have not heard from the old men, fire-worshiping."

The prophet of good omen knew
That the old man, of State become ruined, was a Guebre.

He drove him away with contempt when he saw him a
 stranger to Islam;
For to the pure the filthy is forbidden.

The angel Surosh came from the glorious Omnipotent,
With majesty, reproaching, saying: "Oh, friend of God!

"I had for a hundred years given him victuals and life;
Abhorrence of him comes to thee in a moment.

"If he takes his adoration to the fire,
Why withdrawest thou thy hand of magnanimity?"

I know not who told me this tale,
That there had been, in the country of Yaman, an order-giver.

He snatched the ball of empire from those renowned;
For in treasure-bestowing there was no equal to him.

One could call him "the Cloud of Liberality,"
For his hand used to scatter money like rain.

No one used to take to him the name of (mention) Hatim,
At which (mentioning), frenzy used not to go to his head,

Saying: "How much — of the words of that wind-weigher,
Who has neither country, nor command, nor treasure?"

I heard that he prepared a royal feast,
And harp-like entertained the people, in the midst of the banquet.

One opened the door of mention of Hatim;
Another began to utter his praise.

Envy held the man to the desire of revenge;
He appointed one for his blood-devouring,

Saying: "So long as Hatim is in my time,
"My name will not go into the world for goodness."

The calamity-seeking one took the path to the tribe of Tai,
He set out for the slaying of the young man.

There came before him on the road a young man,
From whom the perfume of affection came up to him:

Good of visage, and wise, and sweet of tongue;
He brought him a guest, that night, to his own abode:

Exercised liberality, and sympathized, and made excuses;
Snatched the enemy's heart by kindness:

Placed the morning-kiss on his hands and feet,
Saying: "Stay at ease, a few days, with us."

He said: "I can not here become a resident;
For I have before me an important matter."

He replied: "If thou wilt reveal the matter to me
I will with soul exert myself, like friends of one heart."

He replied: "Oh young man! listen to me;
For I know the generous one is a secret-concealer.

"Thou knowest, perhaps, in this land, Hatim,
Who is of happy judgment and good manners?

"The King of Yaman has desired his head;
I know not what hatred has arisen between them.

"Show me the short path to where he is;
Oh friend! this indeed I look for from thy courtesy."

The youth laughed, saying: "I am Hatim:
Behold! separate with the sword the head from my body.

"When the morning becomes white it is not proper that
Injury should reach thee, or that thou shouldst become disappointed." [2]

When Hatim placed, with nobleness, his head for slaughter,
A cry issued from the young man (the guest).

He fell upon the dust, and leaped to his feet;
Kissed now the dust; now his feet and hands:

Threw down the sword, and placed the quiver on the ground;
Put, like the helpless, his hands on his breast,

Saying: "If I strike a rose on thy body,
I am, in men's sight, a woman, not a man."

He kissed both his eyes, and embraced him;
And took his way thence to Yaman.

Between the two eyebrows of the man, the King
Knew immediately that he had not performed the duty.

[2] "My relatives may do thee an injury for slaying me; therefore slay me at once, and get thee away."

He said: "Come; what news hast thou?
Why didst thou not bind his head to thy saddle-strap?

"Perhaps a renowned one made an assault against thee;
Thou, through weakness, sustainedst not the fury of the contest?"

The clever youth gave the ground-kiss;
Praised the King; and the majesty of his nature,

Saying: "I discovered Hatim, fame-seeking,
Skilful, and of pleasant appearance, and of good visage:

"Considered him generous and endowed with wisdom;
Regarded him, in manliness, my superior:

"The load of his favor made my back bent;
He slew me with the sword of kindness and grace."

Whatever he experienced, from his liberality — he uttered;
The monarch recited praises on the offspring of Tai:

Gave the envoy gold-money,
Saying "Liberality is the seal on Hatim's name."

It (the evidence) reaches (touches) him, if they give evidence;
Since truth and fame are his fellow travelers.

I have heard that in the time of the Prophet the tribe of Tai
Made not acceptance of the faith of the Koran.

The Messenger of good news and the Observer (Mohammed) sent an army;
They took captive a multitude of them.

The Prophet ordered them to slay them with the sword of hate,
Saying: "They are unclean, and of impure religion."

A woman said: "I am Hatim's daughter,
Ask pardon for me from this renowned Ruler (Mohammed):

"Oh revered sir! exercise generosity as to my state;
For my lord Hatim was endowed with liberality."

By the command of the Prophet of pure judgment,
They loosed the fetters from her hands and feet:

Drew the sword upon the rest of that tribe,
So that they caused, mercilessly, a torrent of blood to flow.

With weeping the woman said to the swordsman:
"Strike my neck also with all the rest:

"I consider not release from fetters, generosity;
I — alone; and my friends in the noose of calamity."

She kept uttering lamentations over the brothers of Tai;
Her voice came to the Prophet's ear.

The rest of that tribe he gave to her,
Saying: "One of true origin never erred!"

From Hatim's storehouse, an old man
Demanded ten diram's weight of sugar-candy.

From the historian I remember news such
That he sent him a sack of sugar.

The wife said from the tent: "What is this?
The old man's need was exactly ten dirams."

The man-cherisher of Tai heard this speech;
He laughed, and said: "Oh heart's ease of Hai!

"If he demanded what was suitable to his own need, and got it,
Where is the liberality of the offspring of Hatim?"

I have heard that a man experienced house-vexation
For a wasp made a nest in his roof.

His wife said: "What thou desirest in respect to them do not,
Lest that they should become scattered from their native country."

The wise man went to his own work;
The wasps began, one day, to sting his wife.

About the door, and roof, and street — the foolish wife
Kept making lamentation. But the husband said:

"Oh woman! make not thy face bitter toward men;
Thou didst say: 'Slay not the poor wasps!'"

How may one do good to the bad!
Forbearance to ill-doers increases ill.

When thou beholdest a people's injury in a chief,
Cut his throat with a sharp sword.

What dog, in short, is there — for whom they place a victual-tray?
Order that they give him a bone.

How well has the old man of the village (Firdausi) expressed this proverb:
"The baggage-animal, leg-striking (kicking), is best under a heavy load."

If the watchman shows mercy,
No one is able to sleep at night for thieves.

In the circle of contest the spear-reed
Is more precious than a hundred thousand sugar-reeds (canes).

Not every one is worthy of property;
This one requires property; that one, rebuke.

When thou cherishest the cat it takes away the pigeon;
When thou makest the wolf fat it rends Joseph.[3]

The edifice that has not firm foundations —
Make it not lofty; and if thou dost, tremble for it.

How well said Bahram,[4] desert-dwelling,
When his thoroughbred, restive steed threw him to the earth,

"It is proper to take from the herd another horse
Which it is possible to restrain, if he becomes restive."

O son! bind the Euphrates at low-water,
For when the torrent is risen it is of no use.

When the filthy wolf comes to thy snare,
Slay; if not, pluck up thy heart from love for the sheep.

From Iblis adoration never comes;
Nor from the bad jewel — goodness into existence.

Give neither place nor opportunity to the malignant one;
The enemy in the pit, and the demon in the glass bottle — is best.

Say not: "It is proper to kill this snake with a stick";
Strike when he has his head beneath thy stone.

The pen striker (penman) who did ill to his inferiors,
To make, with the sword, his hand a pen (to sever it) — is best.

3 The brothers cast Joseph into a pit, sold him, and represented to their father that a wolf had devoured him.

4 Bahram was called Bahram Ghor, *Sahra-nishin*, because he loved the hunting of asses in the desert.

The deliberator who introduces bad regulations
Takes thee, that he may give thee to hell-fire.

Say not: "For the country this deliberator is enough";
Call him not deliberator who is unfortunate.

The fortunate one acts upon Sadi's speech,
Because it is the cause of increase of country, and deliberation, and judgment.

Chapter III

ON LOVE

Oh happy the time of those distraught in love of Him,
Whether they experience the wound (of separation) or the plaster (of propinquity to Him)!

Beggars from royalty fleeing;
In the hope of union with Him, in beggary, long-suffering.

Time to time they drink the wine of pain (of love for Him);
And if they consider it bitter, they draw breath (are patient).

In the pleasure of wine there is the evil of head-sickness;
The thorn is the armor-bearer of the rose-branch.

Patience which is in remembrance of Him is not bitter;
For bitterness from a friend's hand is sugar.

His captive desires not release from bonds;
His prey seeks not freedom from the snare.

Sultans of retirement, beggars of Hai!
Stages of God recognizers, foot-trace lost.

Intoxicated with the love of the friend (God), reproach-enduring;
The camel, intoxicated, more easily bears the load.

How may people find the path to their state?
For, like the water of life, they are in darkness.

Like the holy house (Jerusalem) within — full of towers (pomp);
Without — the wall left desolate.

Moth-like, they set fire to themselves;
Silkworm-like, they spin not on themselves a protection.

Mistress in embrace — mistress-seeking;
On the stream-bank, lip dry with thirst.

I say not that as to water they are powerless;
But they are, on the Nile, dropsical.

The love of one, like thyself — of water and clay —
Ravishes patience and heartease.

In wakefulness — enamored of her cheek and mole;
In sleep — foot-bound, in thought of her.

In truth, thou placest thy head (life) at her feet, in such a way
That thou considerest the world, in comparison with her existence, non-existent.

When thy gold comes not to the eye (of approval) of thy mistress,
Gold and dust appear to thee the same.

To thee — desire for another appears not;
For with her — place for another remains not.

Thou sayst: "Her lodging is within my eye";
And if thou closest together the eye —"It is in my heart."

Neither thought of any one, lest thou shouldst become disgraced,
Nor power that thou shouldst, for a moment, become patient.

If she desires thy life, thou placest it on the palm of her hand;
And if she puts the sharp sword on thy head, thou placest thy head in submission.

When love, whose foundation is on desire,
Is to such a degree tumult-exciting and command-issuing,

Hast thou wonder at the travelers of the path of God
That they should be immersed in the sea of truth —

In passion for the Beloved, with soul engaged;
In remembrance of the Friend (God), careless of the world?

In memory of God, they have fled from the world; [1]
So intoxicated with the splendor of the Cupbearer (God) that
they have spilled the wine!

It is impossible to effect their cure with medicine;
For none is acquainted with their pain (of love).

From eternity without beginning, to their ear comes: "Am I
not your God?"
With clamor, in a shout, they utter: "Yes!"

A crowd — office-holding, corner-sitting;
Feet clayey, breath fiery —

Pluck up, with a shout, a mountain from its place;
Heap together, with a cry, a city:

Are wind-like, invisible, and swift-moving;
Are stone-like, silent, but praise-uttering.

In the morning, they weep to such a degree that the water
Washes down from their eyes the collyrium of sleep.

[1] In Sufism *saki*, or wine, signifies "a holy spiritual guide"; and hence God, who, cupbearer-like, gives the wine of love to His lovers, and makes them non-existent in His beauty.

The second line means: "With the splendor of the Cupbearer (God) they are to such a degree intoxicated, and become non-existent, that they have spilled the wine of love, and have no need of wine for causing intoxication (*masti*), and selflessness (*be-khudi*)."

Steed of the body slain, with the great austerity with which
they have urged the night;
In the morning, shouting, saying: "They are wearied!"

Night and day, in the sea of frenzy and burning;
From perturbation they know not night from day.

So enamored of the splendor of the figure-painter (God)
That they have no occupation with the beauty of the outward
form.

The pious ones gave not their hearts to the covering (external
beauty);
And if a fool gave — he is brainless and fleshless.

That one drank the pure wine of the Unity of God,
Who forgot this world and the next.

I have heard that once upon a time one, beggar-born,
Had affection for one king-born.

He went, and cherished a vain desire;
Imagination plunged its teeth in desire.

Mile-stone like, he used not to be free (absent) from his (the
prince's) plain;
Bishop-like, at all times, at the side of his horse.[2]

His heart became blood, and the secret remained in his heart;
But his feet, through weeping, remained in the mire of desire.

The guards obtained intelligence of his grief;
They said to him: "Wander not again here!"

A moment, he went; recollection of the friend's face came to
him;
Again he pitched his tent, at the head of his friend's street.

[2] At chess, the bishop is next the knight (horse).

A slave broke his head, and hand, and foot,
Saying: "Said we not once to thee — come not here?"

Again to him patience and rest remained not;
On account of his friend's face, patience remained not.

Like flies from off the sugar, with violence him
They used to drive away; but with speed he used to return.

One said to him: "Oh, impudent one of insane appearance!
Thou hast wonderful patience as to blows of stick and stone."

He said: "This violence against me is through his tyranny;
It is not proper to complain of a friend's hand.

"Behold, I express the breath of friendship
If he holds me friend; or, if enemy,

"Expect not, without him, patience from me;
Nay — even with him, repose has no possibility.

"Neither the power of patience, nor room for anger;
Neither the possibility of being (stopping), nor the foot of
flight.

"Say not — turn aside the head from this door of the Court;
Though he place my head, like a tent-peg in the tent-rope.

"Nay — the moth, life given at its friend's foot,
Is better than alive in its dark corner."

He said: "If thou shouldst suffer the wound of his club?"
He replied: "I will fall at his feet, ball-like."

He said: "If, with the sword, he cuts off thy head?"
He replied: "This much even I grudge not.

"To me — indeed, there is not so much knowledge —
Whether the crown or the axe be at my head.

"Display not reproof with me impatient;
For patience appears not in love.

"If my eye becomes white (diseased) like Yakub,[3]
I abandon not hope of seeing Yusuf.

"One who is happy (in love) with another
Is not vexed with him for every little thing."

One day the youth kissed his (the prince's) stirrup;
He became angry; and turned the rein from him.

He laughed, and said: "Turn not the rein;
For the Sultan turns not away the rein (face) from any.

"To me — by thy existence, existence remains not;
To me — in memory of thee, self-worshiping remains not.[4]

"If thou observest a crime, reproach me not:
Thou art head brought forth (produced) from my collar (of existence).

"I fixed my hand in thy stirrup with that boldness;
For I brought not myself in the account.

"I drew the pen on (effaced) my own name;
Placed my foot on the head of my own desire.

"The arrow of that intoxicated eye slays me indeed;
What need that thou should bring thy hand to the sword!

[3] Yakub, or Jacob, from much weeping for Yusuf, or Joseph, became blind; he still kept the hope of seeing him. The meeting eventually took place.

[4] Whenever the degree of love reaches the perfection of exaltation, there is in the lover's heart no room for another. To such a degree does this occur, that the lover forgets his own existence, and considers himself indeed the beloved one. Thus Majnum, in fancy of Laila, regarded his own body as Laila, and said, "I am Laila!" The beggar, even so, regarded his own body to be that of his beloved, and recognized not himself.

"Set fire to the reed, and pass;
So that in the forest neither dry nor green thing may remain."

I have heard that at the chanting of a singer
One of Pari face began to dance.

From the fire of the distracted hearts around her
A candle-flame caught in her skirt.

She became troubled in heart and vexed;
One of her lovers said: "What fear?

"Oh love! as to thee — the fire burned the skirt;
As to me — it burned, all at once, the harvest (of existence)."

If thou art a lover, express not a breath about thyself;
For it is infidelity to speak of lover and one's self.

I recollect hearing from a knowing old man in this way,
That one, distraught with love, turned his head to the desert.

The father, through separation from him, neither ate nor slept;
They reproached the son; he said:

"From that time, when Friend called me one of his own,
Further love for any one remained not to me.

"By God! when He showed me His beauty,
Whatever else I beheld appeared to me fancy."

He who turned away from the people became not lost;
For he found again his own lost one (God).

There are beneath the sky shunners of men,
Whom one can call, at once, wild beast and also angel.

Like the angel, they rest not from remembering the King (God);
Like the wild beast they, night and day, shun men.

Strong of arm (by spirituality); but short of hand (by materiality);
Wise — outwardly mad; sensible — outwardly intoxicated.

Sometimes tranquil in a corner, religious habit-stitching;
Sometimes perplexed in society, religious habit-burning.

Neither passion as to themselves; nor solicitude for any one;
Nor place for any one, in the cell of their unitarianism.

Perturbed of reason, confused of sense;
Ear-stuffed to the word of the adviser.[5]

The duck will not become drowned in the river (of lust);
The samundar! [6] what knows he of the torment of burning?

Empty of hand, men of full stomach (proud);
Desert wanderers, without a Kafila:

They have no expectation of the people's approbation;
For they are approved of God; and that is enough.

Dear ones of God concealed from the people's eye;
Not those waist-cord-possessing, clothed in the habit of the dervish.

They are full of fruit, and shady, vine-like;
Are not like us — of black deeds, and blue garment-dyers.[7]

Head plunged in themselves (in reflection), oyster-like;
Not foam (on mouth) gathered, river-like.

[5] The adviser is one who tries to lead them to the world.

[6] The samundar, or salamander, traditionally dwells in the fire; when it comes forth from the fire, it dies. Sultans make caps of its skin.

[7] In former times, Sufis wore blue-colored woolen garments.

If wisdom be thy friend, be afraid of them (those foam-gathered);
For they are demons in the garb of men.

They are not men indeed of bone and skin;
A true soul is not in every form.

The Sultan (God) is not the purchaser of every slave;
Not beneath every religious garment is there a living man.

If every drop of hail had become a pearl,
The bazar would have become full of them like small shells.

A person said to a moth: "Oh contemptible one!
Go; take a friend suitable to thyself,

"Go on such a path, that thou mayst see the way of hope;
Thou, and the love of the candle is from where to where?

"Thou art not the samundar; circle not around the fire;
For, manliness is first necessary for man, then conflict.

"The blind mouse (bat) goes hidden from the sun;
For force is foolish against an iron grasp.

"The person whom thou knowest to be thy enemy,
To take for a friend is not the part of wisdom."

No one says to thee: "Thou dost do good
When thou placest thy life in the desire of his love.

"The beggar who, of a king, asked (in marriage) for his daughter,
Suffered pushing on the back of his head, and nurtured a vain passion.

"How may she bring into reckoning a lover like thee,
For the faces of kings and sultans are toward her?

"Think not that, in such an assembly, she
Will exercise courtesy to a poor one like thee.

"Or if she practise gentleness toward the whole creation —
Thou art a helpless one — she will exercise severity to thee."

Behold! the ardent moth
What it said: "Oh wonder-displayer! if I burn, what fear?

"Like Ibrahim, a fire of love is in my heart,
That thou mayst consider this candle-flame is to me a rose.[8]

"My heart draws not the skirt of the ravishing one (the candle);
But its love draws the collar of my soul.

"Voluntarily I take not myself to the fire;
But the chain of love is about my neck.

"Even so, I was far, when it burned me;
Not this moment, when the fire of love kindled in me.

"A beloved one, in regard to loveliness, does not do that,
That one can speak to her of continence.

"Who reproaches me for love of the friend,
When, slain at the friend's foot, I am content?

"Knowest thou why I have a lust for destruction,
When it (the candle) is, if I am not — it is proper.

"I will burn because it is the approved beloved,
In whom, the burning of the friend (the moth) makes circulation.

"How long speakest thou to me, saying: 'Suitable to thyself
Get a companion, compassionate to thyself'?

[8] Nimrod threw Ibrahim, or Abraham, into the fire. God made the fire a rose-garden for Ibrahim's sake.

" Admonition to that one of distraught state is as if
Thou shouldst say to one scorpion-bitten — lament not!

" Oh, astonished one! utter not advice to that person
In whom thou knowest that it will take no effect.

" To the helpless one, rein-gone from the hand,
They say not: ' O boy! urge slowly.' "

How pleasantly occurred this witticism in the book Sindbad:
" O son! love is fire; advice, wind."

The fierce fire, by the wind, becomes more lofty;
The panther, by striking, becomes more angry.

When I saw, thoroughly thou doest evil
That thou placest my face opposite to one like thyself.

Seek one better than thyself, and reckon it gain;
For, with one like thyself, thou losest time.

The self-worshipers go in pursuit of such as themselves;
Those intoxicated of God go in a dangerous street (of love).

When I first possessed desire for this work,
I took up, at once, my heart from desire (of life).

One head-casting is true as a lover;
For one of white-liver is the lover of himself.

Death, in ambush, suddenly slays me;
It is better, indeed, that the delicate one should slay me.

When, doubtless, destruction is written on my head,
Destruction is most pleasant by the hand of the beloved.

Dost thou not, one day, in helplessness, yield the soul?
Then it is best thou surrender it at the feet of the beloved.

One night I recollect that my eyes slept not;
I heard that a moth spoke to a candle,

Saying: "I am a lover; if I burn, it is lawful,
Wherefore is thy weeping and burning?"

It replied: "Oh, my poor lover!
Honey (wax), my sweet friend, has departed from me.

"When sweetness (wax) goes away from me,
Like (the statuary) Farhad, fire goes to my head."

The candle kept speaking — and every moment a torrent of grief
Ran down on its yellow cheeks —

Saying: "Oh claimant! love is not thy business;
For thou hast neither patience nor the power of standing.

"Thou dost fly from before a naked flame;
I am standing until I completely burn.

"If the fire of love burns my feathers,
Behold me, whom it burns from head to foot.

"Observe not my splendor, assembly-illuminating;
Consider the heat and torrent of my heart-burning.

"Like Sadi, whose outward form is illuminated;
But, if thou lookest, his vitals are burned."

A portion of the night, even so, had not passed,
When one of Pari-face suddenly extinguished it.

While its smoke rose to its head, it kept saying:
"Oh, son! this is indeed the end of love!"

This is the way of God, if thou wilt learn;
By being slain, thou wilt obtain ease from the burning (of love).

Make not lamentation over the grave of one slain by the friend;
Say: "Praise be to God! that he is accepted by Him."

If thou art a lover, wash not the hand of sickness (of love).
Wash the hand, like Sadi, of worldly design.

The one who sacrifices his life keeps not his hand from his object,
Though they rain arrow and stone on his head.

I said to thee, "Beware; go not to the ocean;
But if thou goest, entrust thy body to the storm."

[Chapters IV and V deal with Humility and Resignation.]

Chapter VI

ON CONTENTMENT

He knew not God and worshiped not,
Who displayed not contentment with his fortune and daily food.

Contentment makes a man rich;
Inform the greedy one, world-traveling:

Oh, one without permanence! bring tranquillity to thy hand.
For vegetation grows not on the rolling stone.

If thou art a man of judgment and sense, cherish not thy body;
For when thou cherishest it, thou slayest it.

Wise men are skill-cherishers;
But body-cherishers are feeble in skill.

Eating and sleeping is the way of beasts alone;
To be in this way is the habit of the unwise.

That one attended to a manly life
Who silenced first the dogs of lust.

Happy that fortunate one who, in a corner,
Gathers to his hand road-provisions of the knowledge of God.

Those to whom God's mystery became revealed
Preferred not the false to it.

But when he knows not darkness from light,
Whether the sight of a demon, or the cheek of a houri — to him what difference?

Thou didst cast thyself into a well, on that account,
That thou didst not recognize the well from the road.

How may the young hawk fly to the zenith of the sky
When, in its long feathers, the stone of desire is bound?

If from lust's claw, thy skirt free
Thou shouldst make, thou wouldst go to the lotus-tree (in Paradise).

By eating less food than one's custom,
One can make the body of angelic temperament.

How may the brutal lion reach the angel state?
It can not fly from earth to sky.

Practise first the human temperament;
Think after that of the angelic temperament.

Thou art on the flanks of a refractory colt;
Take care that it twist not its head from thy order.

For if it should tear the halter from thy hand,
It would slay thy body and spill thy blood.

If thou art a man, eat food within limit;
Such a full belly! — art thou a man, or a jar?

Within the body is a place for food, and reflection on God, and breath;
Thou thinkest it is for bread only.

In the wallet of lust, where is remembrance of God contained?
With difficulty he breathes — leg extended.

The body-cherishers have no knowledge
That the full stomach is void of wisdom.

The two eyes and stomach became not filled with anything;
These bowels, coil on coil, are best empty.

Like hell which they fill with fuel,
Again there is a shout, saying: "Is there any more?"

Thy 'Isa (the soul) continually dies of weakness;
Thou art in that desire that thou mayst cherish thy ass (the body).

Oh, one of little worth! buy not the world in exchange for religion;
Purchase not thou the ass with the gospel of 'Isa.

Perhaps thou seest not that as to rapacious and non-rapacious animals,
Only the greed of eating casts into the snare.

The panther, which stretches its neck (in pride) among the beasts,
Falls, mouse-like, into the snare, through the greed of eating.

Mouse-like, whose bread and cheese thou eatest,
Into his snare thou fallest and sufferest his arrow.

If food be delicious, or if it be simple,
When delay occurs to thy hand, thou eatest pleasantly.

The sage places his head on the pillow at that time when
Sleep takes him, with violence, into its net.

So long as thou obtainest not the power of speech, speak not;
When thou seest not the plain (of power), beware of the ball (of speech).

Speak not; and so long as thou canst, plant not thy foot
Outside of limit, or inside of limit.

Go; acquire a pure heart;
The belly will not become full, save with the dust of the grave.

A Haji gave me an ivory comb,
Saying: "May the mercy of God be on the good qualities of
pilgrims!"

I heard that once upon a time he had called me a dog,
For his heart was, in some way, dejected about me.

I threw away the comb, saying: "This bone,
Is unnecessary for me; another time, call me not a dog.

"Think not, if I swallow my own vinegar,
That I will endure the violence of the lord of sweetmeats."

O soul! be content with a little
That thou mayst consider the sultan and the dervish as one.

Why goest thou before the king with entreaty?
When thou placest avarice aside, thou art a king.

And if thou art a self-worshiper, make the belly a drum;
Make the door of this and that man a Kibla.

And if every moment thy lust says, give!
It causes thee to wander, village to village, in beggary.

Oh, man of sense, contentment exalts the head;
The head full of avarice comes not forth from the shoulder.

A certain one possessed of avarice, before King Khwarazm
— I heard — went early in the morning.

When he saw Khwarazm he became doubled and straight;
He rubbed his face, moreover, on the earth, and arose.

His son said: "Oh little father, name-seeking!
I ask of thee a difficulty; explain it.

"Didst thou not say that the dust of Hijaz was thy Kibla?
Why didst thou to-day pray in this direction (toward the King)?"

Display not devotion to the lust of the lust-worshiper;
Since it has every hour another Kibla.

Avarice spilled the reputation of honor;
It poured out a skirt full of pearls for two barley-grains.

When thou wishest to become satiated with the rivulet-water,
Why spillest thou face-water (honor) for the sake of ice?

Perhaps thou art a patient one as to happiness;
But if not thou art, of necessity, begging at doors.

Sir! go; make short the hand of avarice;
What need to thee of the long sleeve of beggary?

Of him who folded up the casket of avarice
It is unnecessary to write: "Slave or servant to any one."

Expectation will drive thee from every assembly;
Drive it from thyself, so that no one may drive thee.

To one of the holy men a fever came,
A person said: "Ask for sugar from such a one."

He said: "Oh, son! the bitterness of my dying
Is better than my bearing the oppression of one of bitter face."

The wise man ate not sugar from the hand of that one
Who, through arrogance, made his face vinegar (bitter) toward him.

Go not in pursuit of whatever thy heart desires,
For the strengthening of the body diminishes the soul's light.

Imperious lust makes a man contemptible;
If thou art wise, hold it not dear.

If thou enjoyest whatever may be thy wish,
Thou wilt endure much disappointment from the revolution of time.

To heat constantly the oven of the belly
May, in the day of want, be a misfortune.

In straitened circumstances thy face causes not its complexion to be shed
If, in the time of plenteousness, thou makst the belly tight.

The man, full-devourer, endures the belly-load;
And if he obtain not food, he endures the grief-load.

Thou mayst often see the belly-slave greatly ashamed,
In my opinion the belly straitened is better than the heart straitened.

Alas! thou art one man-born, full of dignity,
Who is like the beasts —" Nay; they are lost!"

Show not pity to the ox of great weight,
For it is a great sleeper and great devourer.

If fatness, ox-like, be necessary to thee,
Submit thy body, ass-like, to the tyranny of persons.

Knowest thou what wonderful thing I brought from Basra? —
A tale, which is sweeter than the green date.

We — a few individuals in the religious garb of the true (Sufis) —
Passed by the side of a date-garden.

One among us was a stomach-barn (a glutton);
He was, through this narrow-eyedness, a belly-enjoyer.

The wretched one bound his loins and ascended the date-tree;
And thence fell heavily headlong.

The Ra'is of the village came, saying: "Who slew this man?"
I said: "Express not against us a harsh word.

"The belly drew his skirt down from the branch."
The one of narrow heart is of capacious bowels.

Not every time can one eat the date and carry it away;
The stomach-barn (the glutton) suffered a bad end, and died.

The belly is the hand-fetter and foot-chain;
A belly-slave rarely worships God.

The locust is assuredly altogether belly;
The ant of small belly drags the locust by the foot.

A certain one had sugar-cane, on a small plate —
A wanderer, left and right, for a purchaser.

In a corner of the village, to a pious man, he spoke,
Saying: "Take; and pay when thou hast the means."

That wise man of adorned disposition uttered
An answer, that should be written on the eye.

"Perhaps, to thee, patience (as to payment) may not be exercised toward me;
But to me patience is as to the sugar-cane."

Sugar in its reed has no sweetness
When behind it is the bitter demand for its price.

To one of the men of illumined mind
The Amir of Khutan gave a piece of silk cloth.

He expanded, through gladness, like the laughing rose-leaf;
Kissed his hands, clothed himself, and said:

"How good is the garment of honor of the King of Khutan!
But my own religious garment is more beautiful than it."

If thou art noble, sleep on the earth; for it is enough;
Perform no one's ground-kiss (in obeisance) for a costly carpet.

A certain one had no bread-food, save an onion;
He had no resources and means, like others.

One said to him: "Oh, one of foolish time!
Go; bring something cooked from the tray of plunder (the king's table).

"Oh sir! ask, and have fear of none;
For the one ashamed is cut as to his victuals."

He bound about him his overcoat, and quickly folded his hand (sleeve);
They rent his coat, and broke his hand.

I have heard that he said, while he wept blood:
"What is the remedy for the deed done by one's self!

"The captive of avarice is one calamity-seeking,
After this — I and my house, bread and onion are enough."

The barley-loaf, which I eat by the power of my arm,
Is better than flour twice sifted on the tray of people of liberality.

Last night how heart-straitened slept that worthless one
Who kept the ear of expectation upon the Kibla of others!

In an old woman's house there was a certain cat
Which was of reversed fortune and of bad state.

It went running to the Amir's guest-house;
The slaves of the sultan struck it with arrows.

It ran, blood dropping from its bones (wounds),
While from fear of life it ran, it kept saying:

"If I escape from the hand of this arrow-caster,
I and the mouse and the old woman's desolate abode are enough."

Oh, my soul! honey is not worth the sting's wound;
Contentment with one's own syrup of dates is best.

The Lord God is not satisfied with that slave
Who is not content with his Lord's portion.

. . . . .

Chapter VII

ON EDUCATION

The language of this chapter is on integrity, and deliberation,
and disposition;
Not on the steed, and the battle-field, and the ball-game.

Thou art fellow-lodger with the enemy — lust;
Why art thou a stranger in the art of conflict?

Those turning back the rein of lust from forbidden things
Surpassed Rustem and Sam in manliness.

Chastise thyself with a stick, boy-like;
Beat not men's brains with the heavy mace.

No one has concern for an enemy like thee
Who prevailest not against thy own body.

Thy body is a city full of good and bad;
Thou art sultan; and wisdom is the prime minister.

Know for sure that the mean, neck-exalting,
In this city are — pride and passion and avarice.

Resignation and the fear of God are the free of good report;
Lust and concupiscence are highwaymen and cut-purses.

When the sultan displays favor to the bad,
How may ease remain for the wise?

Lust and avarice and pride and envy
Are like blood in thy veins; and like the soul in thy body.

If these enemies should obtain nurture,
They would turn aside their heads from thy order and judgment.

On the part of lust and concupiscence, opposition remains not
When they experience the grasp of sharp wisdom.

The Ra'is who punished not the enemy
Ruled not also — by reason of the enemy's power.

What need to say much in this chapter
When a word is enough, if a person acts upon it?

If thou bringest thy feet mountain-like (firmly) beneath thy skirt,
Thy head will pass beyond the sky in grandeur.

There was a young man, skilful and learned,
Who was, as regards admonishing, vigilant and manly.

Of good repute, and pious, and God-worshiping,
The beard of his face more beautiful than his handwriting.

Strong in eloquence, and clever in grammar;
But he used not to utter truly the letters of the Abjad.

Perhaps he had stammering in the tongue,
For he used not to explain the truth of the Mu'jam.

I spoke to one of the pious,
Saying: "A certain one has no front teeth."

At my folly he became red of face,
Saying: "Speak not again in this foolish way.

"Thou didst see in him that very defect which is existent;
From how much skill thy wisdom's eye was shut!

"Listen truly to me; for in the day of certainty (Resurrection),
The man, good-seeing, will not experience evil.

"One who has grace, and science, and judgment —
If the foot of his integrity slips from its place.—

"Approve not violence against him, for one small matter.
What have the sages said: Take what is clean."

Oh wise man! the thorn and the rose are together:
Why art thou in the fetter of the thorn? fasten thou the rose-bouquet.

He in whose nature is the ugly disposition
Sees not the peacock — only his ugly foot.

O one of malevolent face! acquire purity of heart;
For the dark mirror displays not the face.

Seek a path by which thou mayst escape from punishment of hell;
Not a word of man, on which thou mayst lay the finger of criticism.

O wise one! place not in front (expose not) the people's defects;
For it sews up thy eyes from thy own defects.

Why do I inflict punishment on the one of stained skirt
When I know, within myself, that I am of wet (stained) skirt?

It is improper that thou shouldst exercise violence against a person
When thou dost aid thyself by artifice of speech.

When evil is unpleasant to thee, do not do it thyself;
Say, after that, to thy neighbor: "Do not evil."

If I am God-worshiping, or if self-displaying,
I preserve my exterior for thee, my interior for God.

When I adorned my exterior with chastity,
Interfere not with my crookedness, or uprightness.

If my way of life be good, or if bad,
God is more acquainted than thou with my secret.

Punish for bad conduct that person
Who hopes from thee the reward of goodness.

If I am good or bad, be thou silent;
For I am myself the porter of profit and loss.

For a good deed by a man of good judgment —
For one, God writes ten.

O son! of whomsoever thou also a single talent
Mayst observe, pass by his ten defects.

Count not upon the finger one defect of his;
Bring forth a world of excellence for nothing.

Like the enemy, who, on the poetry of Sadi,
Glances with scorn, heart ruined —

He has no ear for the hundred beautiful subtleties;
When he beholds a defect, he raises a shout.

That one, bad-approving — to whom there is only this reason —
Envy plucked out his eyes, good-discerning.

Did not God's creating create the people?
Black, and white, and beautiful, and ugly — came.

Not every eye nor eyebrow that thou seest is good;
Eat the kernel of the pistachio-nut; cast away its husk.

Chapter VIII

ON THANKS

I can not express a breath for thanks to my Friend (God);
For I know not a word of praise that is worthy of Him.

Every hair on my body is a gift from Him;
How may I perform thanks for every hair?

Praise to the Lord-Giver
Who, from nonentity, made the slave existing.

To whom is there the power of description of His beneficence?
For His praises are immersed in His dignity.[1]

That inventor who creates a person from clay
Gives soul and wisdom and sense and heart.

From the father's back-bone to the limit of old age,
Behold to what extent He, from the unseen, gave thee honor!

When God created thee pure, be sensible and pure;
For it is a shame to go unclean to the dust of the grave.

Shake off continually the dust of mean qualities from the mirror of the heart;
For it takes not polish when the blight eats it.

In the beginning, wast thou not water of man's seed?
If thou art a man, put presumption out of thy head.

When thou bringest, with effort, victuals to thyself,
Rely not on the strength of thy own arm.

[1] If one utters thanks to God,
How may he utter thanks for the grace of thanks to God?

Oh self-worshiper! why dost thou not see God
Who brings into revolution the arm of the hand?

When by thy striving, a thing happens,
Know by God's grace it is; not by thy own effort.

By violence no one has carried off the ball;
Utter praise to the Lord of Grace.

Of thyself, thou art not erect one step;
From the hidden, aid arrives momently.

Wast thou not a child, tongue-bound as to boast (of speech)?
Food from the navel kept coming within thee.

When they severed the umbilical cord, thy daily food was broken off;
Thy hand clung to thy mother's breast.

A traveler, before whom adverse time brings sickness,
They give to him water from his own city, as medicine.[2]

Then he obtained nourishment in the belly;
He obtained food from the store of the bowels.

The two breasts — that to-day are heart-pleasing to him —
Are also two fountains of his nurturing-place.

The bosom and breast of the mother, heart-pleasing,
Are paradise; and the breast is for him a stream of milk.

Her stature, life-nourishing, is a tree;
The offspring on her bosom — a delicate fruit.

Are not the veins of the breast within the heart?
Then if thou wilt consider, milk is the heart's blood.

[2] It is said that when a person drinks the water of his native place, he obtains convalescence.

Teeth, sting-like, plunged in her blood;
Love for her own blood-devourer created within her.

When God made the arm strong; and the teeth dense —
The nurse anoints her breast with aloes.

The aloe makes it (the offspring) silent (forgetful) of milk, so
That it forgets the breast and its milk.

Oh sir! thou also art, as to repentance, a child of the path of God;
By bitterness, sin becomes forgotten by thee.

A young man turned his head from his mother's judgment,
Her sorrowful heart burned like fire.

When she became helpless she brought a cradle before him,
Saying: "Oh, one languid of love and forgetful of the time of infancy!

"Wast thou not weeping, and tired and small,
When nights, from thy power, sleep overpowered me not?

"No; to thee in the cradle there was not the strength of thy present state;
To thee there was not the power to drive away a fly from thyself.

"Thou art that one who used to be vexed with a single fly,
Who, to-day, art chief and powerful."

Thou mayst again be in that state, at the bottom of the grave,
When thou canst not repel an ant from thy body.

Again how may the eye light up its lamp,
When the worm of the grave devours the fat of the brain?

Like one clothed as to the eye (blind), seest thou not that the road
He knows not, at the time of going, from the well?

Thou who art possessed of vision, if thou didst perform thanks (knowest the path from the well);
If not, thou also art one clothed as to the eye (blind).

The instructor taught thee not understanding and judgment;
God created these qualities in thy existence.

If He had refused thee a heart, truth-hearing,
Truth would have appeared to thy eye the essence of falsehood.

Behold one finger, with how many joints,
God, by creating, cast together.

Then it is madness and foolishness
That thou shouldst place thy finger (of caviling) on the word of His creating.

For the sake of man's motion consider
Him who fixed the sinews and placed the articulations of so many bones.

For without the revolution of the ankle, and the knee, and the foot,
It is impossible to raise the foot from its place.

Prostration (on the ground) is not difficult for a man, on that account,
That, the joint in his back-bone is not of one piece.

God has arranged two hundred joints within one another,
Who has finished like thee, oh, God! a clay-joint?

Oh, one of agreeable disposition! the veins in thy body
Are a land — in it are three hundred and sixty streams.

In the head — vision, and thought, and judgment, and discretion;
The limb of the body for the dear heart; and the heart for dear wisdom.

The wild beasts with the countenance downcast, are contemptible;
Thou, *Alif*-like, art a rider on thy feet.

They, head-lowered, for the sake of eating;
Thou, with dignity, bringest thy food to the head.

It beseems thee not, with so much chieftainship,
That thou shouldst lower thy head, save in devotion to God.

By His own beauty God gave thee knowledge; behold!
He made thee not, like the animals, head in the grass.

But with this form, heart-enchanting,
Be not fascinated; take a good walk of life.

A straight path is necessary, not erect stature;
For the infidel is also like us in outward form.

He who gave thee eye and mouth and ear;
If thou art wise — strive not in opposition to Him.

I grant that thou mayst beat the enemy with a stone,
Wage not war, at least from ignorance, with the Friend (God).

Those of wise disposition, obligation-recognizing,
Sew up the favor of God with the nail of thanks.

A certain one severely rubbed a boy's ears (chastised him),
Saying: "Oh father of wonderful judgment, of overturned fortune!

"I gave thee an axe, saying: Split firewood;
I said not: Undermine the masjid-wall!"

The tongue came from God for thanks and praise;
The grateful one moves it not in slander.

The ear is the thoroughfare for the Koran and counsel;
Strive not to listen to calumny and falsehood.

Two eyes, for the sake of beholding the creating of God, are good;
Lower the eyes from the defect of brother and friend.

For the sake of thy ease the night and day are;
The resplendent moon and the sun, world-illuminating.

For thy sake the west wind, chamberlain-like,
Causes constantly to be spread the carpet of spring.

If wind, and snow, and rain, and hail are,
And if the Chaugan expresses thunder, and the sword lightning —

All are work-performers, and order-bearers of God
Who cherish thy seed in the dust.

And if thou remainest thirsty, rage not through affliction;
For the Water-carrier brings thee a cloud of water on His back.

From the dust He brings color, and perfume, and food;
Amusement for the eye, and brain, and palate.

He gave thee honey from the bees, and manna from the sky;
He gave thee the green date from the date-tree, and the date-tree from the seed-stone.

All the gardeners gnaw the hand
In astonishment, saying: "No one planted such a date-tree!"

The sun and moon and Pleiades, all are for thee;
They are the candles of the roof of thy house.

He brings thee a rose from the thorn, musk from the animal's navel,
Gold from the mine, and the green leaf from the dry wood.

He portrayed thy eye and eyebrow, with His own hand;
For one can not leave the intimate friend to strangers.[3]

The powerful One who cherishes the delicate
Cherishes thee with various favors.

Breath by breath, with soul, it is proper to utter praise;
For thanks to Him is not a work of the tongue only.

O God! my heart became blood, and eye wounded,
When I see thy reward is greater than my speech of thanksgiving.

I speak not of the rapacious and non-rapacious beast, and ant, and fish,
But of the army of angels above heaven's summit.

Yet they have uttered a little Thy praise;
They have uttered one out of so many thousands which they should have uttered.

Oh Sadi! go; wash thy hand, and the book;
Hasten not on the path that has no end.

A person knows not the value of a day of pleasure,
Save on that day when he falls to hardship-enduring.

[3] By strangers are meant angels. "Thou, an intimate friend of God's, art not left to the angels."

The winter-season of the dervish, in the narrow year —
How easy is it to the lord of wealth?

One healthy who, once complaining, slept not,
Uttered not thanks to God for sound health.

When thou art a manly mover, and swift of foot,
Stand, with thanks to God by those slow of foot.

The young man bestows to the ancient old man;
The powerful one displays pity for the powerless.

What do the people of the Jihun know of the value of water? —
Ask those wearied utterly in the sun.

To the Arab who is sitting by the Tigris
What care is there as to the thirsty ones of the desert of Zarud?

That one recognized the value of healthiness
Who once helpless sweltered in fever.

How may the dark night appear long to thee
Who rollest from side to side in comfort?

Think of one falling and rising in fever;
For the sick one knows the lengthiness of the night.

At the sound of the drum the rich man becomes awake;
What knows he how the watchman passed the night?

I have heard that Tughril, one night in the autumn,
Passed a Hindu watchman,

From the pouring of snow, and rain, and torrent,
Fallen to trembling, like the star Canopus.

His heart, from pity for him, suffered agitation;
He said: "Behold! put on my fur garment.

"Wait a moment, by the terrace-side;
For I will send it out by the hand of a slave."

He was in this speech; and the morning-breeze blew.
The monarch entered the royal hall.

He had in his retinue a slave of Pari-form
For whom his disposition had a little inclination.

The sight of the beloved chanced so agreeably to him
That the wretched Hindu passed from his memory.

The word "fur-coat" passed to his (the watchman's) ear,
It came not, through misfortune, to his shoulders.

Perhaps the torment of toil was not enough for him,
Since the sky's revolution added to it expectation.

When the sultan slept in carelessness, behold
What the watchman said to him in the morning!

"Perhaps the watchman Nek-Bakht was forgotten by thee
When thy hand went to the bosom of the slave-girl Aghosh.

"For thee, the night passes in ease and joy;
As to us, what knowest thou how the night passes?"

One of a caravan, head-lowered to the caldron —
To him, what care of those sunk in sand?

Oh Lord of the Zaurak! keep on the water;
For the water has passed over the head of those helpless.

Oh, vigorous young men! stay;
For in the caravan are sluggish old men.

Thou hast slept well in the *haudaj* of the caravan —
The camel-rein in the camel-driver's hand.

Whether plain or mountain; whether stone or sand — to thee what matter?
Ask the state of the road from those lagging behind.

The camel of burden, mountain-form, carries thee;
What knowest thou of the footman, who devours the blood of grief?

Those sleeping in comfort of heart in the house,
What know they of the state of the hungry belly?

One of naked body made loan of one diram;
He made for his body a garment of rawhide.

He complained, saying: "Oh, perverse fortune!
I am cooked with heat, within this rawhide."

When the uncooked (foolish) one, with fierceness, began to boil —
One from the prison-pit said to him: "Silence!

"Oh raw one! offer thanks to God,
That thou art not like me — rawhide (bound) on hand and foot."

A certain one passed by a holy man,
He came to his sight in the form of a Jew.

He struck him a blow on his neck;
The dervish gave him his shirt.

He became ashamed saying: "What passed from me was a fault.
Pardon me; what room (need) is there for giving a shirt?"

He said: "On this shirt-giving I am firm, in thanks to God,
That that one whom thou didst think me, I am not."

One left behind on the road was weeping,
Saying: "Than I in this desert, who is more wretched?"

An ass, load-carrier, said to him: "Oh, one without discretion!
How long bewailest thou also of the tyranny of the heavens?

"Go; thank God although thou art not on an ass,
That thou art, in short, a son of Adam, not an ass."

A lawyer passed by one fallen drunk;
He became proud of his own abstinence.

Through haughtiness he looked not at him;
The young man raised his head, saying: "Oh, old man!

"Go; thank God, when thou art in prosperity,
For disappointment comes from pride.

"Laugh not at one whom thou seest in bonds;
Lest that suddenly thou shouldst fall into confinement.

"In short, is it not in the possibility of fate
That thou mayst be to-morrow fallen drunk like me?"

. . . . . .

Chapter IX

ON REPENTANCE

Oh, thou whose age has passed to seventy years! Come;
Thou wast, perhaps, asleep, that thy life went to the wind.

Thou didst prepare every requisite of being in this world;
Didst not engage thyself in the thought of going to the next world?

On the Resurrection-day, when they lay out the market of heaven,
They give dignities for good deeds.

Stock in trade, as much as thou bringest thou takest away;
And if thou art poor, thou takest away shame.

For the more full the market, just so much
The more distressed is the heart of the one of empty hand.

If out of fifty dirams five become wanting,
Thy heart, with the grasp of grief, becomes torn.

When fifty years have gone forth from thy hand,
Consider it gain that there is a space of five days.

If the wretched corpse had possessed a tongue
He would have raised a shout in lament and cry,

Saying: "Oh living one! when there is the power of speech
Let not the lip sleep (cease), corpse-like, from uttering the name of God.

"Since our time, in carelessness passed,
Do thou, at least, reckon a few moments — opportunity."

One night, in youth and the pleasure of affluence (of youth),
We, young men, sate sometime together.

Nightingale-like, singing; rose-like, fresh of face;
From hilarity, clamor cast into the street.

An old man, world-experienced, apart from us,
The blackness of his hair white, through the violence of Time,

Was tongue-bound, as to speech, nut-like;
Was unlike us, lip from laughter, pistachio-nut-like.

A youth went before him, saying: "Oh, old man!
Why sittest thou with sorrow in the corner of regret?

"Raise once thy head from the collar of grief;
Move jauntily, with ease of heart, with the young men."

He year-stricken raised his head from concealment;
Behold his answer! how like an old man he spoke:

"When the morning breeze blows over the garden
It befits the young tree to move to and fro.

"The green corn, so long as it is young and the head green, waves;
When it reaches mellowness it becomes broken.

"In the spring-time, when the wind brings the fragrance of the musk-willow,
The ancient tree sheds its dry leaves.

"It does not beseem me to move jauntily with young men
When the morning of old age has blossomed on my cheek.

"The male falcon of my soul, which was within my bonds,
Wishes, from time to time, to snatch the end of the thread of life.

"Yours is the time to sit at this tray of enjoyment;
For we have washed our hands of luxurious enjoyment.

"When the dust of venerability sits on the head,
Look not again for the pleasure of youth.

"Snow rained on my raven feathers (hair),
The spectacle of the garden, nightingale-like, is not suitable
to me.

"The peacock, possessed of beauty, makes display;
What desirest thou of the hawk, feather-stripped?

"For me, the reaping of the corn is near;
For you, now the fresh verdure of the beard grows.

"The freshness of our rose-garden has passed;
Who binds the rose-bouquet when it has become withered?

"Oh, soul of father! my reliance is on a staff;
Further reliance on life is a mistake.

"For the young man it is reserved to leap on his feet;
For old men prefer a request for aid to the hands of others.

"Behold the red rose of my face — pure yellow;
When the sun becomes yellow it descends.

"To entertain lust, on the part of an immature youth,
Is not so odious as on the part of an old man.

"It is proper for me to weep, like children,
For shame of my sins; not to live, childlike in sport."

Lokman spoke well saying: "Not to live
Is better than to live years in sin."

Even to shut the shop-door in the morning
Is better than to give from the hand (to squander) the profit
and capital of life.

While the young man causes the blackness (of hair) to attain
to light (whiteness),
The wretched old man takes his whiteness to the grave.

Oh bone-cage! knowest thou
That thy soul is a bird; and its name spirit?

When the bird departs from the cage of the body, and snaps
its chain,
It becomes not, by effort, again thy prey.

Take care of opportunity; for the world is for a moment;
In the opinion of the wise, a moment of life is better than a
world.

Sikandar, who held sway over a world,
Abandoned the world, at that time when he died.

To him it was unattainable that — a world from him
They might take; and give him, in return, a moment's respite.

They departed, and every one reaped what he sowed;
There only remains — good and bad name.

Why place we the heart on this caravan-place,
From which friends have departed; and we are on the road?

After us — the garden gives this very rose;
Friends sit with one another.

Fix not the heart on this mistress of the world;
For she sate with no one whose heart she ravished not.

I remember, in my father's time —
The rain of mercy, every moment on him! —

That he purchased in my childhood a tablet and book;
He bought for my sake also a gold ring.

Suddenly a purchaser took off
The ring from my hand for a single date.

When the little boy understands not the value of a ring,
They can take it away from him for a sweetmeat.

Thou also didst not recognize life's value
When thou didst throw it away for sweet ease.

On the Resurrection-day, when the good attain to the highest dignity,
They rise from the bottom of the grave-ashes to the Pleiades.

Thy head will, from shame, remain lowered before thee,
When thy bad deeds arise around thee.

Brother! have shame of the work of the bad;
For thou wilt become ashamed in the presence of the good.

On that day, when they ask of thy deeds and words,
The body of the lords of resolution (the prophets) will tremble from fear.

In the place where the prophets suffer fear,
Come, what excuse for sin, hast thou?

. . . . . .

Chapter X

ON PRAYER

Come; let us raise a hand from the heart;
For to-morrow (after death), one can not raise the hand from
the clay of the grave.

In the autumn season, seest thou not the tree
Which, from severe cold, remains leafless!

It uplifts the empty hands of supplication.
It returns not, through God's mercy, empty-handed (leafless).

Fate gives to it a renowned dress of honor;
Destiny places fruit within its bosom.

At that door, which God never closed — think not
That he, hands raised in supplication, becomes hopeless.

All bring devotion; and the wretched, supplication;
Come, so that at the Court of the Cherisher of the Wretched
(God)

We may raise the hand, like the naked (leafless) branch;
For one can not sit longer than this without means (leafless).

Oh Lord! look with bounty
When sin comes into existence (issues) from Thy slaves.

Sin issues from the dust-like slave,
In hope of the pardon of the Lord.

O Merciful One! we are cherished by Thy bounty;
We are accustomed to Thy favor and grace.

When a beggar experiences liberality, and grace, and tenderness,
He turns not back from the rear of the giver.

Since Thou didst make us precious in the world,
We have expectation of this same dearness in the future world.

Thou alone givest preciousness and despicability;
One dear to Thee experiences contempt from none.

O God! by Thy honor, make me not contemptible in the future world;
By the baseness of sin, make me not ashamed.

Make not a person like unto myself ruler over me;
If I bear punishment it is best from Thy hand.

There is no evil in the world worse than this —
To suffer oppression from the hand of one like unto myself.

Shame of Thee is for me enough;
Make me not further ashamed before any.

If a shadow from Thee falls on my head,
For me the sky is of the lowest rank.

If Thou grantest a crown, it exalts my head;
Raise Thou me, so that none may cast me down.

My body trembles when I bring to recollection
The prayers of one distraught, in the sacred enclosure at Mecca,

Who, with much lamentation, was saying to God:
"Cast me not away; for no one takes my hand.

"Call me with kindness to Thy door; or drive me from Thy door —
My head is only at Thy threshold.

"If Thou knowest that we are wretched and helpless;
We are wearied of imperious lust.

"This headstrong lust hastens to such a degree
That reason can not seize its rein.

"Who, by force, prevails over lust and Shaitan?
The battle-ranks of panthers come not from the ant.

"Give me a path, by the holy men of Thy path,
Give me protection from these enemies (lusts).

"O God! by the nature of Thy Lordship,
By Thy qualities, matchless and unequaled,

"By — I await Thy command — of the pilgrim of the holy
house (the Kaaba),
By the buried Mohammed — peace be on him!

"By the extolling of Thee of men, sword-exercising,
Who reckon the man of war, a woman.

"By the worship of old men adorned with devotion,
By the truth of young men, newly risen —

"I pray, saying: In that whirlpool of a breath (death-
throes),
Help us from the shame of saying, two Gods.

"There is hope from those who perform devotions;
For they make intercession for those devotionless.

"Keep me far from pollution, by the pure;
And hold me excused if any sin passes from me.

"By the old men, back bent with devotion;
Eye from shame of sin stitched to the back of the foot.

"I pray saying: Close not my eye from the face of happiness;
Bind not my tongue at the time of witnessing.

"Hold the lamp of truth opposite my path;
Keep my hand short of doing evil.

"Cause my eyes to turn from that unfit to be seen;
Give me no power, as to disgraceful deeds.

"I am that atom, standing in Thy air,
My existence, on non-existence, through despicability, is one.[1]

"A single ray of the sun of Thy grace is sufficient;
For no one sees me, save in Thy effulgence.

"Glance at the evil one, that he may be better;
A glance from the king is enough for the beggar.

"If Thou, in justice and equity, seizest me,
I will complain, saying: Thy pardon gavest not to me this condition.

"O God! drive me not in contempt from Thy door;
For no other door appears to me.

"And if I become, through ignorance, absent a few days,
Shut not the door in my face when I return.

"What excuse may I bring for the shame of wet-skirtedness,
Unless I offer submission, saying: O independent One!

"I am a poor man; take me not in crime and sin;
The rich man has pity for the poor.

"Why is it necessary to weep for the weakness of my state?
If I am weak, my shelter is Thou.

[1] A mote, from the sun's effulgence and moon's luminosity, becomes visible; in obscurity, its existence and non-existence are one.

"O God! in carelessness, we broke the covenant;
What force may the hand of struggle bring against destiny?

"What issues from the hand of our deliberation?
This reliance is, indeed, enough — confession of our sin.

"Whatever I did, Thou didst strike it all together (upset it);
What power may one's self exert against God?

"I take not my head beyond Thy order;
But Thy command thus passes over my head."

A certain one called one of blackish color, ugly;
He gave to him an answer of such a sort that he remained astonied.

"I have not created my own form,
"Which thou considerest my fault, saying: I have done ill.

"If I am ugly of face, what business (O sneerer!) hast thou with me?
I am not, in short, the portrayer of the ugly and beautiful."

Beyond that which Thou didst write on my forehead,
Oh Slave-cherisher! I did neither less nor more.

Thou art, in short, the Knower that I am not powerful;
Thou art absolutely powerful — who am I?

If Thou art my Guide, I arrive at safety;
But if Thou shouldst lose me, I remain behind in journeying.

If the World-Creator affords not assistance,
How may the slave exercise abstinence?

How well said the dervish of short hand,
Who, in the night, vowed; and, in the morning, broke his vow:

"If He gives repentance, it will remain steadfast;
For our covenant is unstable and languid."

By Thy truth! stitch up my eyes from falsehood;
By Thy light! consume me not, to-morrow, in hell.

My face, through poverty, went into the dust;
My sin's dust ascended to Heaven.

Oh, Cloud of Mercy! rain Thou once;
For dust, in the presence of rain, remains not.

Through sin, to me, in this kingdom of the world is no rank;
But to the next world there is no path.

Thou knowest the intention of those tongue-bound;
Thou placest the plaster on those heart-wounded.

An idolater was door shut as to his face against the world;
He was loin-girt in an idol's service.

After some years, as to that one of despised religion,
Fate brought before him a difficult matter.

At the idol's foot, in the hope of good,
He helplessly rolled, in the dust of the temple,

Saying: "O idol! I am distressed; help me;
I am ready to die; pity my body."

Many times, in its service, he groaned;
But any deeds for his arrangement issued not.

How may an idol accomplish a person's important affairs,
Which can not drive a fly from its face?

He was confounded, saying: "Oh, one foot-bound in error!
I worshiped thee several years, in folly:

"Accomplish the important matter which I have before me;
Otherwise I will ask it from the Omnipotent."

His face, still stained with dust from (prostration before) the idol,
When the pure God accomplished his wish.

One truths-recognizing became astonished at this;
For his pure time became to him obscured —

Saying: "A mean, false, perturbed worshiper,
His head still with the wine of the wine-tavern intoxicated —

"Washed not his heart from infidelity; nor his religion from treachery —
God fulfilled that desire which he sought!"

His heart descended into this difficulty,
When a message from God came to the ear of his heart,

Saying: "The old man of deficient wisdom, before the idol,
Uttered much; but his prayer was unacceptable.

"If he be also repulsed from Our Court,
Then from the idol to the Lord God — what difference?"

Oh, friend! it is necessary to bind the heart on the Lord God;
Than the idol whatever (or whosoever) it be — who are more helpless?

If thou placest thy head in devotion at this door, it is impossible,
That the hand of need should return to thee empty.

O God! we came deficient in work;
We came empty of hand, but hopeful.

I have heard that one intoxicated with the heat of the date-wine
Ran to the most sacred place of a *masjid.*

He bewailed at the threshold of mercy,
Saying: " O Lord! take me to the loftiest Paradise! "

The Mu'azzin seized his collar, saying: " Make haste,
O one careless of wisdom and religion! — a dog and a *masjid.*

" What worthy deed didst thou, that thou seekst Paradise?
Grace beseems thee not with an ugly face."

The old man uttered this speech, while the intoxicated one wept,
Saying: " Oh sir! I am drunk; keep thy hand from me.

" Hast thou wonder at the grace of the Omnipotent,
When a sinner is hopeful?

" I say not to thee (oh Mu'azzin!) — accept my excuse;
The door of repentance is open, and God is helper."

I have constantly shame of the grace of the Merciful One;
For I call my sin great, in comparison with his pardon.[2]

When old age brings down a person from his feet —
When thou seizest not his hand, he rises not from his place.

I am that old man, fallen from his feet;
O God! help me, by Thy own grace.

I say not: Give me greatness and rank;
Pardon me the cause of my wretchedness (sin), and my crime.

[2] The author here begins to speak.

If a friend knows a little defect regarding me
He makes me notorious for foolishness.

Thou seeing, and we fearful of each other;
For Thou art the Screen-coverer of sin, and we the screen-render.

Men from without the screen have raised a shout on finding a defect;
Thou art always within the screen and screen-coverer.

If slaves, in foolishness, turn their heads from order,
The lords draw the pen (efface the crime).

If Thou pardonest sin to the extent of Thy liberality,
There remains no captive in existence.

And if Thou becomest angry to the extent of sin —
Send to hell; and ask not for the balance.

If Thou helpest me, I may arrive at the appointed place;
And if Thou castest me down — no one assists.

Who uses violence, if Thou givest assistance?
Who seizes, when thou givest deliverance?

In the place of assembling there will be two parties;
I know not which path they may assign to me.

If my road be from the right hand — it is wonderful;
For only crookedness arose from my hand.

My heart gives, time to time, hope,
That God has shame of my white hair.[3]

I have wonder if He has shame of me,
For shame comes not to me of myself.

[3] In the traditions it is stated: "Him, who became old in Islam, God is ashamed to punish."

Did not Yusuf — who experienced such calamity and imprisonment
When his command became current and his rank lofty —

Pardon the crime of the offspring of Ya'kub?
For a good appearance has virtue.

He imprisoned them not for their bad conduct;
He rejected not their small capital.

We also, from Thy grace, have expectation of this very treatment,
Oh, dear One! forgive the sin of this one, without capital.

No one has seen one of blacker deeds than me
Of whom no deed is approved.

Besides this that to me there is hope of Thy assistance;
To me there is hope of Thy forgiveness.

I have brought no capital, save hope;
O God! make me not hopeless of pardon.

THE GULISTAN[1]

Chapter I

OF THE CUSTOMS OF KINGS

I

I have heard of a king who made the sign to put a captive to death. The poor wretch, in that state of desperation, began to abuse the king in the dialect which he spoke, and to revile him with asperity, as has been said; whoever shall wash his hands of life will utter whatever he may harbor in his heart:

"When a man is desperate he will give a latitude to his tongue,
Like as a cat at bay will fly at a dog"

—"at the moment of compulsion when it is impossible to fly, the hand will grasp the sharp edge of a sword." The king asked, saying, "What does he say?" One of the Viziers (or nobles in attendance), and a well-disposed man, made answer, "O my lord! he is expressing himself and saying,

"Paradise is for such as are restraining their anger
And forgiving their fellow-creatures; and God will befriend the benevolent."

The king felt compassion for him, and desisted from shedding his blood. Another nobleman, and the rival of that former, said, "It is indecorous for such peers, as we are, to use any language but that of truth in the presence of kings; this man abused his majesty, and spoke what was unworthy of him." The king turned away indignant at this remark, and replied, "I was better pleased with his falsehood than with this truth that you have told; for that bore the face of good policy, and this was founded in malignity; and the intelligent have

[1] Translated by James Ross.

said, 'A peace-mingling falsehood is preferable to a mischief-stirring truth': Whatever prince may do that which he (his counselor) will recommend, it must be a subject of regret if he shall advise aught but good."

They had written over the portico of King Feridun's palace: "This world, O brother! abides with none. Set thy heart upon its maker, and let him suffice thee. Rest not thy pillow and support on a worldly domain which has fostered and slain many such as thou art. Since the precious soul must resolve on going, what matters it whether it departs from a throne or the ground?"

II

One of the kings of Khorassan saw, in a dream, Sultan Mahmud, the son of Saboktagin, a hundred years after his death, when his body was decayed and fallen into dust, all but his eyes, which as heretofore were moving in their sockets and looking about them. All the learned were at a stand for its interpretation, excepting one dervish, who made his obeisance, and said: "He is still looking about him, because his kingdom and wealth are possessed by others! — Many are the heroes whom they have buried under ground, of whose existence above it not one vestige is left; and of that old carcass which they committed to the earth, the earth has so consumed it that not one bone is left. Though many ages are gone since Nushirowan was in being, yet in the remembrance of his munificence is his fair renown left. Be generous, O my friend! and avail thyself of life, before they proclaim it as an event that such a person is not left."

III

I have heard of a king's son who was short and mean, and his other brothers were lofty in stature and handsome. On one occasion the king, his father, looked at him with disparagement and scorn. The son, in his sagacity, understood him and said, "O father! a short wise man is preferable to a tall blockhead; it is not everything that is mightier in stature that is superior in value:

"A sheep's flesh is wholesome, that of an elephant carrion.
Of the mountains of this earth Sinai is one of the least,
Yet is it most mighty before God in state and dignity.

Heardst thou not what an intelligent lean man said one day to a sleek fat dolt? An Arab horse, notwithstanding his slim make, is more prized thus than a herd of asses."

The father smiled; the pillars of the State, or courtiers, nodded their assent, and the other brothers were mortified to the quick. Till a man has declared his mind, his virtue and vice may have lain hidden; do not conclude that the thicket is unoccupied, peradventure the tiger is gone asleep!

I have heard that about that time a formidable antagonist appeared against the king. Now that an army was levied in each side, the first person that mounted his horse and sallied upon the plain was that son, and he exclaimed: "I can not be that man whose back thou mayest see on the day of battle, but am him thou mayest descry amidst the thick of it, with my head covered with dust and blood; for he that engages in the contest sports with his own blood, but he who flees from it sports with the blood of an army on the day of fight." He so spoke, assaulting the enemy's cavalry, and overthrew some renowned warriors. When he came before the king he kissed the earth of obeisance, and said, "O thou, who didst view my body with scorn, whilst not aware of valor's rough exterior, it is the lean steed that will prove of service, and not the fatted ox, on the day of battle."

They have reported that the enemy's cavalry was immense, and those of the king few in number; a body of them was inclined to fly, when the youth called aloud, and said, "Be resolute, my brave men, that you may not have to wear the apparel of women!" The troops were more courageous on this speech, and attacked altogether. I have heard that on that day they obtained a complete victory over the enemy. The king kissed his face and eyes, and folded him in his arms, and became daily more attached to him, till he declared him heir-apparent to the throne. The brothers bore him a grudge, and put poison into his food. His sister saw this from a window, and closed the shutter; and the boy understood the sign, and withdrew his hand from the dish, and said, "It is hard that the virtuous should perish and that the vicious should occupy their places." Were the *homayi,* or phœnix, to be extinct in the world, none would take refuge under the shadow of an owl. They informed the father of this event; he sent for the brothers and rebuked them, as they deserved. Then he made a division of his domains, and gave a suitable portion to each, that discontent might cease; but the ferment was increased, as they have said: Ten dervishes can sleep on one rug, but two kings can not be accommodated in a whole kingdom. When a man after God's heart can eat the moiety of his loaf, the other moiety he will give in alms to the poor. A king may acquire the sovereignty of one climate or empire; and he will in like manner covet the possession of another.

IV

A horde of Arab robbers had possessed themselves of the fastness of a mountain, and waylaid the track of the caravan. The yeomanry of the villages were frightened at their stratagems, and the king's troops alarmed, inasmuch as they had secured an impregnable fortress on the summit of the mountain, and made this stronghold their retreat and dwelling.

The superintendents of the adjacent districts consulted together about obviating their mischief, saying: If they are in this way left to improve their fortune, any opposition to them may prove impracticable. The tree that has just taken root, the strength of one man may be able to extract; but leave it to remain thus for a time, and the machinery of a purchase may fail to eradicate it: the leak at the damhead might have been stopped with a plug, which now it has a vent we can not ford its current on an elephant.

Finally it was determined that they should set a spy over them, and watch an opportunity when they had made a sally upon another tribe, and left their citadel unguarded. Some companies of able warriors and experienced troops were sent, that they might conceal themselves in the recesses of the mountain. At night, when the robbers were returned, jaded with their march and laden with spoil, and had stripped themselves of their armor, and deposited their plunder, the foremost enemy they had to encounter was sleep. Now that the first watch of night was gone: "the disk of the sun was withdrawn into a shade, and Jonas had stepped into the fish's mouth"— the bold-hearted warriors sprang from their ambush and secured the robbers by pinioning them one after another.

In the morning they presented them at the royal tribunal, and the king gave an order to put the whole to death. There happened to be among them a stripling, the fruit of whose early spring was ripening in its bloom, and the flower-garden of his cheek shooting into blossom. One of the viziers kissed the foot of the imperial throne, and laid the face of intercession on the ground, and said, "This boy has not yet tasted the fruit of the garden of life, nor enjoyed the fragrance of the flowers of youth: such is my confidence in the generous disposition of his Majesty that it will favor a devoted servant by sparing his blood." The king turned his face away from this speech; as it did not accord with his lofty way of thinking, he replied: "The rays of the virtuous can not illuminate such as are radically vicious; to give education to the worthless is like throwing walnuts upon a dome: it were wiser to eradicate the tree of their wickedness, and annihilate their tribe; for to put out a fire and leave the embers, and to kill a viper and foster its young, would not be the acts of rational beings. Though the clouds pour down the water of vegetation, thou canst never gather fruit from a willow twig. Exalt not the fortune of the abject, for thou canst never extract sugar from a mat or common cane."

The vizier listened to this speech; willingly or not he approved of it, and applauded the good sense of the king, and said: "What his majesty, whose dominion is eternal, is pleased to remark is the mirror of probity and essence of good policy, for had he been brought up in the society of those vagabonds, and confined to their service, he would have followed their vicious courses. Your servant, however, trusts that he may be instructed to associate with the virtuous, and take to the habits of the prudent; for he is still a child, and the lawless and refractory principles of that gang can not have yet tainted his mind; and it is in tradition that —

Whatever child is born, he is verily born after the right way, namely Islamism,
Afterward his father and his mother bring him up as a Jew, Christian, or Gueber.

The wife of Lot associated with the wicked, and her posterity failed in the gift of prophecy; the dog of the seven sleepers (at Ephesus) for some time took the path of the righteous, and became a rational being."

He said this, and a body of the courtiers joined him in intercession, till the king acceded to the youth's pardon, and answered: "I gave him up, though I saw not the good of it. Knowest thou what Zal said to the heroic Rustem: 'Thou must not consider thy foe as abject and helpless. I have often found a small stream at the fountain-head, which, when followed up, carried away the camel and its load.'"

In short, the vizier took the boy home, and educated him with kindness and liberality. And he appointed him masters and tutors, who taught him the graces of logic and rhetoric, and all manner of courtier accomplishments, so that he met general approbation. On one occasion the vizier was detailing some instances of his proficiency and talents in the royal presence, and saying: "The instruction of the wise has made an impression upon him, and his former savageness is obliterated from his mind." The king smiled at this speech, and replied: "The whelp of a wolf must prove a wolf at last, notwithstanding he may be brought up by a man."

Two years after this a gang of city vagabonds got about him, and joined in league, till on an opportunity he murdered the vizier and his two sons; and, carrying off an immense booty, he took up the station of his father in the den of thieves, and became a hardened villain. The king was apprised of this event; and, seizing the hand of amazement with the teeth of regret, said: "How can any person manufacture a tempered saber from base iron; nor can a base-born man, O wiseacre, be made a gentleman by any education! Rain, in the purity of whose nature there is no anomaly, cherishes the tulip in the garden and common weed in the salt-marsh. Waste not thy labor in scattered seed upon a briny soil, for it can never be made to yield spikenard; to confer a favor on the wicked is of a like import, as if thou didst an injury to the good."

V

At the gate of Oghlamish Patan, King of Delhi, I (namely Sadi) saw an officer's son, who, in his wit and learning, wisdom and understanding, surpassed all manner of encomium. In the prime of youth, he at the same time bore on his forehead the traces of ripe age, and exhibited on his cheek the features of good fortune: "Above his head, from his prudent conduct, the star of superiority shone conspicuous."

In short, it was noticed with approbation by the king that he possessed bodily accomplishments and mental endowments. And sages have remarked that worth rests not on riches, but on talents; and the discretion of age, not in years, but on good sense. His comrades envied his good fortune, charged him with disaffection, and vainly attempted to have him put to death: "but what can the rival effect so long as the charmer is our friend?"

The king asked, saying, "Why do they show such a disinclination to do you justice?" He replied: "Under the shadow of his majesty's good fortune I have pleased everybody, excepting the envious man, who is not to be satisfied but with a decline of my success; and let the prosperity and dominion of my lord the king be perpetual!" I can so manage as to give umbrage to no man's heart; but what can I do with the envious man, who harbors within himself the cause of his own chagrin? Die, O ye envious, that ye may get a deliverance; for this is such an evil that you can get rid of it only by death. Men soured by misfortune anxiously desire that the state and fortune of the prosperous may decline; if the eye of the bat is not suited for seeing by day, how can the fountain of the sun be to blame? Dost thou require the truth? It were better a thousand such eyes should suffer, rather than that the light of the sun were obscured.

VI

They tell a story of a Persian king who had stretched forth the arm of oppression over the subjects' property, and commenced a system of violence and rapacity to such a degree that the people emigrated to avoid the vexatiousness of his tyranny, and took the road of exile to escape the annoyance of his extortions. Now that the population was diminished and the resources of the State had failed, the treasury remained empty, and enemies gathered strength on all sides. Whoever may expect a comforter on the day of adversity, say, let him practise humanity during the season of prosperity; if not treated cordially, thy devoted slave will forsake thee; show him kindness and affection, and the stranger may become the slave of thy devotion.

One day they were reading, in his presence, from the Shah-Nameh, of the tyrant Zohak's declining dominion and the success of Feridun. The vizier asked the king, saying: "Can you so far comprehend that Feridun had no revenue, domain, or army, and how the kingdom came to be confirmed with him?" He answered: "As you have heard, a body of people collected about him from attachment, and gave their assistance till he acquired a kingdom." The vizier said: "Since, O sire, a gathering of the people is the means of forming a kingdom, how come you in fact to cause their dispersion unless it be that you covet not a sovereignty? So far were good that thou wouldst patronize the army with all thy heart, for a king with an army constitutes a principality." The king asked: "What are the best means of collecting an army and yeomanry?" He replied: "Munificence is the duty of a king, that the people may assemble around him, and clemency, that they may rest secure under the asylum of his dominion and fortune, neither of which you have. A tyrant can not govern a kingdom, for the duty of a shepherd is not expected from the wolf. A king that can anyhow be accessory to tyranny will undermine the wall of his own sovereignty."

The advice of the prudent minister did not accord with the disposition of the king. He ordered him to be confined, and immured him in a dungeon. It soon came to pass that the sons of the king's uncle rose in opposition, levied an army in support of their pretensions, and claimed the sovereignty of their father. A host of the people who had cruelly suffered under the arm of his extortion and were dispersed, gathered around and succored them till they dispossessed him of his kingdom and established them in his stead. That king who can approve of tyrannizing over the weak will find his friend a bitter foe in the day of hardship. Deal fairly with thy subjects, and rest easy about the warfare of thine enemies, for with an upright prince his yeomanry is an army.

IX

In his old age an Arab king was grievously sick, and had no hopes of recovery, when lo! a messenger on horseback presented himself at the palace-gate, and joyfully announced, saying: "Under his majesty's good fortune we have taken such a stronghold, made the enemy prisoners of war, and reduced all the landholders and vassals of that quarter to obedience as subjects." On hearing this news the king fetched a cold sigh, and answered: "These glad tidings are not intended for me but for my rivals, namely, the heirs of the sovereignty. My precious life has, alas! been wasted in the hope that what my heart chiefly coveted might enter at my gate. My bounden hope was gratified; yet what do I benefit by that? There is no hope that my passed life can return. The hand of death beats the drum of departure. Yes, my two eyes, you must bid adieu to my head. Yes, palm of my hand, wrist, and arm, all of you say farewell, and each take leave of the other. Death has overtaken me to the gratification of my foes; and you, O my friends, must at last be going. My days were blazed away in folly; what I did not do let you take warning and do."

X

At the metropolitan mosque of Damascus I was one year fervent in prayer over the tomb of Yahiya, or John the Baptist and prophet, on whom be God's blessing, when one of the Arab princes, who was notorious for his injustice, chanced to arrive on a pilgrimage, and he put up his supplication, asked a benediction, and craved his wants.— The rich and poor are equally the devoted slaves of this shrine, and the richer they are the more they stand in need of succor. Then he spoke to me, saying: "In conformity with the generous resolution of dervishes and their sincere zeal, you will, I trust, unite with me in prayer, for I have much to fear from a powerful enemy." I answered him, "Have compassion on your own weak subjects, that you may not see disquiet from a strong foe. With a mighty arm and heavy hand it is dastardly to wrench the wrists of poor and helpless. Is he not afraid who is hard-hearted with the fallen that if he slip his foot nobody will take him by the hand? — Whoever sowed the seed of vice and expected a virtuous produce, pampered a vain brain and encouraged an idle whim. Take the cotton from thy ear and do mankind justice, for if thou refusest them justice there is a day of retribution. The sons of Adam are members one of another, for in their creation they have a common origin. If the vicissitudes of fortune involve one member in pain, all the other members will feel a sympathy. Thou, who art indifferent to other men's affliction, if they call thee a man art unworthy of the name."

XI

A dervish, whose prayers had a ready acceptance with God, made his appearance at Bagdad. Hojaj Yusuf (a great tyrant) sent for him and said: "Put up a good prayer for me." He prayed, "O God! take from him his life!" Hojaj said, "For God's sake, what manner of prayer is this?" He answered: "It is a salutary prayer for you, and for the whole sect of Mussulmans.— O mighty sir, thou oppressor of the feeble, how long can this violence remain marketable? For what purpose came the sovereignty to thee? Thy death were preferable to thy tyrannizing over mankind."

XIII

An unjust king asked a holy man, saying. "What is more excellent than prayers?" He answered: "For you to remain asleep till mid-day, that for this one interval you might not afflict mankind."— I saw a tyrant lying dormant at noon, and said, "This is mischief, and is best lulled to sleep. It were better that such a reprobate were dead whose state of sleep is preferable to his being awake."

XIV

One of the ancient kings was easy with the yeomanry in collecting his revenue, but hard on the soldiery in his issue of pay; and when a formidable enemy showed its face, these all turned their backs. Whenever the king is remiss in paying his troops, the troops will relax in handling their arms. What bravery can be displayed in the ranks of battle whose hand is destitute of the means of living?

One of those who had excused themselves was in some sort my intimate. I reproached him and said, "He is base and ungrateful, mean and disreputable who, on a trifling change of circumstances, can desert his old master and forget his obligation of many years' employment." He replied: "Were I to speak out, I swear by generosity you would excuse me. Peradventure, my horse was without corn, and the housings of his saddle in pawn.— And the prince who, through parsimony, withholds his army's pay can not expect it to enter heartily upon his service."— Give money to the gallant soldier that he may be zealous in thy cause, for if he is stinted of his due he will go abroad for service.

So long as a warrior is replenished with food he will fight valiantly,
And when his belly is empty he will run away sturdily.

XV

One of the viziers was displaced, and withdrew into a fraternity of dervishes, whose blessed society made its impression upon him and afforded consolation to his mind. The king was again favorably disposed toward him, and offered his reinstatement in office; but he consented not, and said, "With the wise it is deemed preferable to be out of office than to remain in place.— Such as sat within the cell of retirement blunted the teeth of dogs, and shut the mouths of mankind; they destroyed their writings, and broke their writing reeds, and escaped the lash and venom of the critics." — The king answered: "At all events I require a prudent and able man, who is capable of managing the State affairs of my kingdom." The ex-minister said: "The criterion, O sire, of a wise and competent man is that he will not meddle with such like matters.— The *homayi,* or phœnix, is honored above all other birds because it feeds on bones, and injures no living creature."

A Tamsil, or application in point.— They asked a *Siyah-gosh,* or lion-provider, "Why do you choose the service of the lion?" He answered: "Because I subsist on the leavings of his prey, and am secure from the ill-will of my enemies under the asylum of his valor." They said: "Now you have got within the shadow of his protection and admit a grateful sense of his bounty, why do you not approach more closely, that he may include you within the circle of select courtiers and number you among his chosen servants?" He replied, "I should not thus be safe from his violence."— Though a Gueber may keep his fire alight for a hundred years, if he fall once within its flame it will burn him.— It on one occasion may chance that the courtier of the king's presence shall pick up a purse of gold, and the next that he shall lie shorter by the head. And philosophers have remarked, saying, "It is incumbent on us to be constantly aware of the fickle dispositions of kings, who will one moment take offense at a salutation, and at another make an honorary dress the return for an act of rudeness; and they have said, That to be over much facetious is the accomplishment of courtiers and blemish of the wise.— Be wary, and preserve the state of thine own character, and leave sport and buffoonery to jesters and courtiers.

XVI

One of my associates brought me a complaint of his perverse fortune, saying, "I have small means and a large family, and can not bear up with my load of poverty. Often has a thought crossed my mind, suggesting, Let me remove into another country, that in whatever way I can manage a livelihood none may be informed of my good or bad luck." — (Often he went asleep hungry, and nobody was aware, saying, "Who is he?" Often did his life hang upon his lip, and none lamented over him.) —"On the other hand, I reflect on the exultation of my rivals, saying, They will scoffingly sneer behind my back, and impute my zeal in behalf of my family to a want of humanity.— Do but behold that graceless vagabond who can never witness the face of good fortune. He will consult the ease of his own person and abandon to distress his wife and children.— And, as is known, I have some small skill in the science of accounts. If, through your respected interest, any office can be obtained that may be the means of quieting my mind, I shall not, during the remainder of life, be able to express my sense of its gratitude."

I replied, "O brother, the service of kings offers a twofold prospect — a hope of maintenance and a fear for existence; and it accords not with the counsel of the wise, under that expectation, to incur this risk.— No tax-gatherer will enter the dervish's abode, saying, Pay me the rent of a field and orchard; either put up with trouble and chagrin, or give thy heartstrings to the crows to pluck."

He said, "This speech is not made as applicable to my case, nor have you given me a categorical answer. Have you not heard what has been remarked, 'His hand will tremble on rendering his account who has been accessory to a dishonest act.— Righteousness will insure the divine favor; I never met him going astray who took the righteous path.'— And philosophers have said, 'Four orders of people are mortally afraid of four others — the revenue embezzler, of the king; the thief, of the watchman; the fornicator, of the eaves-dropper; and the adulteress, of the censor.' But what has he to fear from the comptroller who has a fair set of account-books? —'Be not extravagant and corrupt while in office if thou wishest that the malice of thy rival may be circumscribed on settling thy accounts. Be undefiled, O brother, in thy integrity, and fear nobody; washermen will beat only dirty clothes against a stone.' "

I replied, "The story of that fox suits your case, which they saw running away, stumbling and getting up. Somebody asked him, 'What calamity has happened to put you in such a state of trepidation?' He said, 'I have heard that they are putting a camel in requisition.' The other answered, 'O silly animal! what connection has a camel with you, or what resemblance is there between you and it?' He said, 'Be silent; for were the envious from malevolence to insist that this is a camel, and I should be seized for one, who would be so solicitous about me as to inquire into my case?' And before they can bring the antidote from Irac the person bitten by the snake may be dead. In like manner, you possess knowledge and integrity, discrimination and probity, yet spies lie in ambush, and informers lurk in corners, who, notwithstanding your moral rectitude, will note down the opposite; and should you anyhow stand arraigned before the king, and occupy the place of his reprehension, who in that State would step forward in your defense? Accordingly, I would advise that you should secure the kingdom of contentment, and give up all thoughts of preferment. As the wise have said: "The benefits of a sea voyage are innumerable; but if thou seekest for safety, it is to be found only on shore.' "

My friend listened to this speech; he got into a passion, caviled at my fable, and began to question it with warmth and asperity, saying, "What wisdom or propriety, good sense or morality, is there in this? Here is verified that maxim of the sage, which tells us they are friends alone that can serve us in a jail, for all our enemies may pretend friendship at our own table.—'Esteem him not a friend who during thy prosperity will brag of his love and brotherly affection.' I account him a friend who will take his friend by the hand when struggling with despair, and overwhelmed with misfortune."

I perceived within myself, saying, "He is disturbed, and listens to my advice with impatience"; and, having called the *sahib diwan,* or lord high treasurer, in virtue of a former intimacy that subsisted between us, I stated his case and spoke so fully upon his skill and merits, that he put him in nomination for a trifling office. After some time, having adverted to his kindly disposition and approved of his good management, his promotion was in train, and he got confirmed in a much higher station. Thus was the star of his good fortune in ascension, till it rose into the zenith of ambition; and he became the favorite of his majesty the king, toward whom all turned for counsel, and upon whom all eyes rested their hopes! I rejoiced at this prosperous change of his affairs, and said: "Repine not at thy bankrupt circumstances, nor let thy heart despond, for the fountain of immortality has its source of chaos.

"Take heed, O brother in affliction! and be not disheartened,
For God has in store many hidden mercies.

Sit not down soured at the revolutions of the times, for patience is bitter, yet it will yield sweet fruit."

At that juncture I happened to accompany a party of friends on a journey to Hijaz, or Arabia Petræa. On my return from the pilgrimage to Mecca, he came out two stages to meet me. I perceived that his outward plight was wretched, and his garb that of dervishes. I asked, "How is this?" He replied, "Just as you said, a faction bore me a grudge and charged me with malpractises; and the king, be his reign eternal, would not investigate the truth of that charge, and my old and best friends stood aloof from my defense, and overlooked my claims on our former acquaintance.— When, through an act of God, a man has fallen, the whole world will put their feet upon his neck; when they see that fortune has taken him by the hand, they will put their hands upon their breasts, and be loud in his praise.— In short, I underwent all manner of persecution till within this week, that the tidings of the safe return of the pilgrims reached us, when I got a release from my heavy durance and a confiscation of my hereditary tenements." I said, "At that time you did not listen to my admonition, when I warned you that the service of princes is, like a voyage at sea, profitable but hazardous: you either get a treasure or perish miserably.— The merchant gains the shore with gold in both his hands, or a wave will one day leave him dead on its beach."— Not deeming it generous any further to irritate a poor man's wound with the asperity of reproach, or to sprinkle his sore with the salt of harsh words, I made a summary conclusion in these two verses, and said:—"Wert thou not aware that thou shouldst find fetters on thy feet when thou wouldst not listen to the generous man's counsel? Thrust not again thy finger into a scorpion's hole till thou canst endure the pain of its sting."

XVI

I was the companion of a holy fraternity, whose manners were correct from piety, and minds disciplined from probity. An eminent prince entertained a high and respectful opinion of the worth of this brotherhood, and had assigned it an endowment. Perhaps one of them committed an act unworthy of the character of dervishes; for the good opinion of that personage was forfeited, and the market of their support shut. I wished that I could by any means re-establish the maintenance of my friends, and attempted to wait on the great man; but his porter opposed my entrance, and turned me away with rudeness. I excused him conformably with what the witty have said: "Till thou canst take an introduction along with thee approach not the gate of a prince, vizier, or lord; for the dog and the doorkeeper, on espying a beggar, will the one seize his skirt and the other his collar."

When the favorite attendants of that great man were aware of my situation, they ushered me into his presence with respect, and offered me the highest seat; but in humility I took the lowest, and said: "Permit that I, the slave of the abject, should seat myself on a level with servants."— The great man answered, "My God, my God! what room is there for this speech? Wert thou to seat thyself upon the pupil of mine eye, I would court thy dalliance, for thou art lovely."

In short, I took my seat, and entered upon a variety of topics, till the indiscretion of my friends was brought upon the carpet, when I said: "What fault did the lord of past munificence remark, that his servant should seem so contemptible in his sight? Individually with God is the perfection of majesty and goodness, who can discern our failings and continue to us his support." When the prince heard this sentiment he subscribed to its omnipotence; and, with regard to the stipendiary allowance of my friends, he ordered its continuance as heretofore, and a faithful discharge of all arrears. I thanked him for his generosity, kissed the dust of obeisance, apologized for my boldness, and at the moment of taking my leave, added: "When the fane of the Kaaba, at Mecca, became their object from a far distant land, pilgrims would hurry on to visit it for many farsangs. It behooves thee to put up with such as we are, for nobody will throw a stone at a tree that bears no fruit."

XVIII

A prince inherited immense riches by succeeding to his father. He opened the hand of liberality, displayed his munificence, and bestowed innumerable gifts upon his troops and people. "The brain will not be perfumed by a censer of green aloes-wood; place it over the fire that it may diffuse fragrance like ambergris. If ambitious of a great name, make a practise of munificence, for the crop will not shoot till thou shalt sow the seed."

A narrow-minded courtier began to admonish him, saying, "Verily, former sovereigns have collected this wealth with scrupulosity and stored it advisedly. Check your hand in this waste, for accidents wait ahead, and foes lurk behind. God forbid that you should want it on a day of need.— Wert thou to distribute the contents of a granary among the people, every master of a family might receive a grain of rice; why not exact a grain of silver from each, that thou mightest daily hoard a chamber full of treasure?"

The prince turned his face aside from this speech, so contrary to his own lofty sentiments, and harshly reprimanded him, saying, "A great and glorious God made me sovereign of this property, that I might enjoy and spend it; and posted me not a sentinel, to hoard and watch over it.— Carown perished, who possessed forty magazines of treasure; Nushirowan died not, who left behind him a fair reputation."

XIX

They have related that at a hunting-seat they were roasting some game for Nushirowan, and as there was no salt they were dispatching a servant to the village to fetch some. Nushirowan called to him, saying, "Take it at its fair price, and not by force, lest a bad precedent be established and the village desolated." They asked, "What damage can ensue from this trifle?" He answered, "Originally, the basis of oppression in this world was small, and every newcomer added to it, till it reached to its present extent.— Let the monarch eat but one apple from a peasant's orchard, and his guards, or slaves, will pull up the tree by its root. From the plunder of five eggs, that the king shall sanction, his troops will stick a thousand fowls on their spits."

XX

I have heard of a revenue-collector who would distrain the huts of the peasantry, that he might enrich the treasury of the sovereign, regardless of that maxim of the wise, who have said, "Whoever can offend the Most High, that he may gain the heart of a fellow-creature, God on high will instigate that creature against him, till he dig out the foundation of his fortune.— That crackling in the flame is not caused by burning rue, but it is the sigh of the afflicted that occasions it."

They say, of all animals the lion is the chief; and of beasts the ass is the meanest; yet, with the concurrence of the wise, the burden-bearing ass is preferable to the man-devouring lion. "The poor ass, though devoid of understanding, will be held precious when carrying a burden; oxen and asses that carry loads are preferable to men that injure their fellow-creatures."

The king had reported to him a part of his nefarious conduct. He put him to the rack, and tortured him to death. "Thou canst not obtain the sovereign's approbation till thou make sure of the good-will of his people. Wishest thou that God shall be bountiful to thee, be thou good thyself to the creatures of God."

One who had suffered from his oppression passed him at the time of his execution, and said: "It is not every man that may have the strong arm of high station, that can in his government take an immoderate freedom with the subjects' property. It is possible to cram a bone down the throat, but when it sticks at the navel it will burst open the belly."

XXI

They tell a story of an evil-disposed person who struck a pious good man on the head with a stone. Having no power of revenge, the dervish was keeping the stone by him till an occasion when the sovereign let loose the army of his wrath, and cast him into a dungeon. The poor man went up and flung the stone at his head. The person spoke to him, saying, "Who are you, and why did you throw this stone at my head?" He answered, "I am that poor man, and this is the same stone that you on a certain occasion flung at my head." He said, "Where have you been all this time?" The poor man answered, "I stood in awe of your high station, but now that I find you in a dungeon, I avail myself of the opportunity, as they have said—'Whilst they saw the worthless man in prosperity, the wise thought proper to show him respect. Now thou hast not sharp and tearing nails, it is prudent for thee to defer to engage with the wicked. Whoever grappled with a steel-armed wrist exposed his own silver arm to torture. Wait till fortune can manacle his hands, then beat out his brains to the satisfaction of thy friends.' "

XXV

I have heard that one of the kings of Arabia directed the officers of his treasury, saying, " You will double a certain person's salary, whatever it may be, for he is constant in attendance and ready for orders, while the other courtiers are diverted by play, and negligent of their duty." A good and holy man overheard this, and heaved a sigh and groan from the bottom of his bosom. They asked, saying, " What vision did you see?" He replied, " The exalted mansions of his devoted servants will be after this manner portioned out at the judgment-seat of a Most High and Mighty Deity! — If for two mornings a person is assiduous about the person of the king, on the third he will in some shape regard him with affection. The sincerely devout exist in the hope that they shall not depart disappointed from God's threshold. The rank of a prince is the reward of obedience. Disobedience to command is a proof of rejection. Whoever has the aspect of the upright and good will lay the face of duty at this threshold."

XXVI

They tell a story of a tyrant who bought firewood from the poor at a low price, and sold it to the rich at an advance. A good and holy man went up to him and said, " Thou art a snake, who bitest everybody thou seest; or an owl, who diggest up and makest a ruin of the place where thou sittest. Although thy injustice may pass unpunished among us, it can not escape God, the knower of secrets. Be not unjust with the people of this earth, that their complaints may not rise up to heaven."

They say the unjust man was offended at his words, turned aside his face, and showed him no civility, as they have expressed it (in the Koran):

He, the glorified God, overtook him amidst his sins:

till one night, when the fire of his kitchen fell upon the stack of wood, consumed all his property, and laid him from the bed of voluptuousness upon the ashes of hell torments. That good and holy man happened to be passing and observed that he was remarking to his friends, "I can not fancy whence this fire fell upon my dwelling." He said, "From the smoke of the hearts of the poor! — Guard against the smoke of the sore-afflicted heart, for an inside sore will at last gather into a head. Give nobody's heart pain so long as thou canst avoid it, for one sigh may set a whole world into a flame."

They have related that these verses were inscribed in golden letters upon Kai-khosrau's crown: "How many years, and what a continuance of ages, that mankind shall on this earth walk over my head. As the kingdom came to me from hand to hand, so it shall pass into the hands of others."

XXVII

A person had become a master in the art of wrestling; he knew three hundred and sixty sleights in this art, and could exhibit a fresh trick for every day throughout the year. Perhaps owing to a liking that a corner of his heart took for the handsome person of one of his scholars, he taught him three hundred and fifty-nine of those feats, but he was putting off the instruction of one, and under some pretense deferring it.

In short the youth became such a proficient in the art and talent of wrestling that none of his contemporaries had ability to cope with him, till he at length had one day boasted before the reigning sovereign, saying, "To any superiority my master possesses over me, he is beholden to my reverence of his seniority, and in virtue of his tutorage; otherwise I am not inferior in power, and am his equal in skill." This want of respect displeased the king. He ordered a wrestling-match to be held, and a spacious field to be fenced in for the occasion. The ministers of State, nobles of the court, and gallant men of the realm were assembled, and the ceremonials of the court marshaled. Like a huge and lusty elephant, the youth rushed into the ring with such a crash that had a brazen mountain opposed him he would have moved it from its base. The master being aware that the youth was his superior in strength, engaged him in that strange feat of which he had kept him ignorant. The youth was unacquainted with its guard. Advancing, nevertheless, the master seized him with both hands, and lifting him bodily from the ground, raised him above his head and flung him on the earth. The crowd set up a shout. The king ordered them to give the master an honorary dress and handsome largess, and the youth he addressed with reproach and asperity, saying, "You played the traitor with your own patron, and failed in your presumption of opposing him." He replied, "O sire! my master did not overcome me by strength and ability, but one cunning trick in the art of wrestling was left which he was reserved in teaching me, and by that little feat had to-day the upper hand of me." The master said, "I reserved myself for such a day as this. As the wise have told us, 'Put it not so much into a friend's power that, if hostilely disposed, he can do you an injury.' Have you not heard what that man said who was treacherously dealt with by his own pupil: 'Either in fact there was no good faith in this world, or nobody has perhaps practised it in our days. No person learned the art of archery from me who did not in the end make me his butt.'"

XXVIII

A solitary dervish had taken up his station at the corner of a desert. A king was passing by him. Inasmuch as contentment is the enjoyment of a kingdom, the dervish did not raise his head, nor show him the least mark of attention; and, inasmuch as sovereignty is regal pomp, the king took offense, and said, "The tribe of ragged mendicants resemble brute beasts, and have neither grace nor good manners." The vizier stepped up to him, and said: "O generous man! the sovereign of the universe has passed by you; why did you not do him homage, and discharge the duty of obeisance?" He answered and said, "Speak to your sovereign, saying: Expect service from that person who will court your favor; let him moreover know that kings are meant for the protection of the people, and not the people for the subjects of kings.— Though it be for their benefit that his glory is exalted, yet is the king but the shepherd of the poor. The sheep are not intended for the service of the shepherd, but the shepherd is appointed to tend the sheep.— To-day thou mayest observe one man proud from prosperity, another with a heart sore from adversity; have patience for a few days till the dust of the grave can consume the brain of that vain and foolish head. When the record of destiny came to take effect, the distinction of liege and subject disappeared. Were a person to turn up the dust of the defunct, he could not distinguish that of the rich man from the poor."

These sayings made a strong impression upon the king; he said: "Ask me for something." He replied: "What I desire is, that you will not trouble me again!" The king said, "Favor me with a piece of advice." He answered: "Attend to them now that the good things of this life are in thy hands; for wealth and dominion are passing from one hand into another."

XXX

A king ordered an innocent person to be put to death. The man said, "Seek not your own hurt by venting any anger you may entertain against me." The king asked, "How?" He replied, "The pain of this punishment will continue with me for a moment, but the sin of it will endure with you forever.— The period of this life passes by like the wind of the desert. Joy and sorrow, beauty and deformity, equally pass away. The tyrant vainly thought that he did me an injury, but round his neck it clung and passed over me."

The king profited by this advice, spared his life, and asked his forgiveness.

XXXI

The cabinet ministers of Nushirowan were debating an important affair of State, and each delivered his opinion according to the best of his judgment. In like manner the king also delivered his sentiments, and Abu-zarchamahr, the prime minister, accorded in opinion with him. The other ministers whispered to him, saying, "What did you see superior in the king's opinion that you preferred it to the judgment of so many wise heads?" He replied: "Because the event is doubtful, and the opinion of all rests in the pleasure of the most high God whether it shall be right or wrong. Accordingly it is safer to conform with the judgment of the king, because if that shall prove wrong, our obsequiousness to his will shall secure us from his displeasure.— To sport an opinion contrary to the judgment of the king were to wash our hands in our own blood. Were he verily to say this day is night, it would behoove us to reply: Lo! there are the moon and seven stars."

XXXII

An impostor plaited his hair and spake, saying, "I am a descendant of Ali"; and he entered the city along with the caravan from Hijaz, saying, "I come a pilgrim from Mecca"; and he presented a Casidah or elegy to the king, saying, "I have composed it!" The king gave him money, treated him with respect, and ordered him to be shown much flattering attention; till one of the courtiers, who had that day returned from a voyage at sea, said, "I saw him on the Eeduzha, or anniversary of sacrifice at Busrah; how then can he be a Haji, or pilgrim?" Another said, "Now I recollect him, his father was a Christian at Malatiyah (Malta); how then can he be a descendant of Ali?" And they discovered his verses in the divan of Anwari. The king ordered that they should beat and drive him away, saying, "How came you to utter so many falsehoods?" He replied, "O sovereign of the universe! I will utter one speech more, and if that may not prove true, I shall deserve whatever punishment you may command." The king asked, "What may that be?" He said: "If a peasant bring thee a cup of junket, two measures of it will be water and one spoonful of it buttermilk. If thy slave spake idly be not offended, for great travelers deal mostly in the marvelous!" The king smiled and replied, "You never in your life spake a truer word." He directed them to gratify his expectations, and he departed happy and content.

XXXIII

They have related that one of the viziers would compassionate the weak and meditate the good of everybody. He happened to fall under the royal displeasure, and they all strove to obtain his release. Such as had him in custody were indulgent in their restraint, and his fellow-grandees were loud in proclaiming his virtues, till the king pardoned his fault. A good and holy man was apprised of these events, and said: "In order to conciliate the good-will of friends, it were better to sell our patrimonial garden; in order to boil the pot of well-wishers, it were good to convert our household furniture into firewood. Do good even to the wicked; it is as well to shut a dog's mouth with a crumb."

XXXIV

One of Haroun-al-Rashid's children went up to his father in a passion, saying, "A certain officer's son has abused me in my mother's name." Haroun asked his ministers, "What ought to be such a person's punishment?" One made a sign to have him put to death; another to have his tongue cut out; and a third, to have him fined and banished. Haroun said: "O my child! it were generous to forgive him; but if you have not resolution to do that, do you abuse his mother in return, yet not to such a degree as to exceed the bounds of retaliation, for in that case the injury would be on our part, and the complaint on that of the antagonist.— In the opinion of the prudent he is no hero that can dare to combat a furious elephant; but that man is in truth a hero who, when provoked to anger, will not speak intemperately. A cross-grained fellow abused a certain person; he bore it patiently, and said, O well-disposed man! I am still more wicked than thou art calling me; for I know my defects better than thou canst know them."

XXXV

I was seated in a vessel, along with some persons of distinction, when a boat sunk astern of us and two brothers were drawn into the whirlpool. One of our gentlemen called to the pilot, saying, "Save those two drowning men and I will give you a hundred dinars." The pilot went and rescued one of them, but the other perished. I observed, "That man's time was come, therefore you were tardy in assisting him, and alert in saving this other." The pilot smiled, and replied, "What you say is the essence of inevitable necessity; yet was my zeal more hearty in rescuing this one, because on an occasion when I was tired in the desert he set me on a camel; whereas, when a boy I had received a horsewhipping from that other."

> God Almighty was all justice and equity:
> Whoever labored unto good experienced good in himself;
> And he who toiled unto evil experienced evil.

So long as thou art able grate nobody's heart, for in this path there must be thorns. Expedite the concerns of the poor and needy; for thy own concerns may need to be expedited.

XXXVII

A person announced to Nushirowan the Just, saying, "I have heard that God, glorious and great, has removed from this world a certain man who was your enemy." He said, "Have you had any intelligence that he has overlooked me? In the death of a rival I have no room for exultation, since my life also is not to last forever."

XXXVIII

At the court of Kisra, or Nushirowan, a cabinet council was debating some State affair. Abu-zarchamahr, who sat as president, was silent. They asked him, "Why do you not join us in this discussion?" He replied, "Such ministers of State are like physicians, and a physician will prescribe a medicine only to a sick man; accordingly, so long as I see that your opinions are judicious, it were ill-judged in me to obtrude a word.— While business can proceed without my interference, it does not behoove me to speak on the subject; but were I to see a blind man walking into a pit, I would be much to blame if I remained silent."

XXXIX

When he reduced the kingdom of Misr, or Egypt, to obedience, Haroun-al-Rashid said, "In contempt of that impious rebel (Pharaoh), who, in his pride of the sovereignty of Egypt, boasted a divinity, I will bestow its government only on the vilest of my slaves." He had a negro bondsman, called Khosayib, preciously stupid, and him he appointed to rule over Egypt. They tell us that his judgment and understanding were such, that when a body of farmers complained to him, saying, "We had planted some cotton shrubs on the banks of the Nile, and the rains came unseasonably, and swept them all away"— he replied, "You ought to sow wool, that it might not be swept away!" A good and holy man heard this, and said: "Were our fortune to be increased in proportion to our knowledge, none could be scantier than the share of the fool; but fortune will bestow such wealth upon the ignorant as shall astonish a hundred of the learned. Power and fortune depend not on knowledge, they are obtained only through the aid of heaven; for it has often happened in this world that the illiterate are honored, and the wise held in scorn. The fool in his idleness found a treasure under a ruin; the chemist, or projector, fell the victim of disappointment and chagrin."

Chapter II

OF THE MORALS OF DERVISHES

I

A person of distinction asked a *parsa,* or devout and holy man, saying, "What do you offer in justification of a certain *abid,* another species of Mohammedan monk, whose character others have been so ready to question?" He replied: "In his outward behavior I see nothing to blame, and with the secrets of his heart I claim no acquaintance.—Whomsoever thou seest in a *parsa's* habit, consider him a *parsa,* or holy, and esteem him as a good man; and if thou knowest not what is passing in his mind, what business has the *mohtasib,* or censor, with the inside of the house?"

II

I saw a dervish who, having laid his head at the fane of the Kaaba of Mecca, was complaining and saying, "O gracious, O merciful God! thou knowest what can proceed from the sinful and ignorant that may be worthy of thy acceptance!—I brought my excuse of imperfect performance, for I have no claim on the score of obedience. The wicked repent them of their sins; such as know God confess a deficiency of worship."

Abids, or the pious, seek a reward of their devotion, merchants a profit on their traffic. I, a devoted servant, have brought hope, not obedience, and have come as a beggar, and not for lucre!

> Do unto me what is worthy of thyself;
> But deal not with me as I myself have deserved.

Whether thou wilt slay me or pardon my offense, my head and face are prostrate at thy threshold. Thy servant has no will of his own; whatever thou commandest, that he will perform. At the door of the Kaaba I saw a petitioner, who was praying and weeping bitterly. I ask not, saying, "Approve of my obedience, but draw the pen of forgiveness across my sins."

III

Within the sanctuary of the Kaaba, at Mecca, I saw Abd-u'l-cadur the Gilani, who having laid his face upon the Hasa, or black stone, was saying, "Spare and pardon me, O God! and if, at all events, I am doomed to punishment, raise me up at the day of resurrection blindfolded, that I may not be put to shame in the eyes of the righteous." Every morning when the day begins to dawn, with my face in the dust of humility, I am saying, "O thou, whom I never can forget, dost thou ever bestow a thought on thy servant?"

IV

A thief got into a holy man's cell; but, however much he searched, he could find nothing to steal, and was going away disappointed. The good soul was aware of what was passing, and taking up the rug on which he had slept, he put it in his way that he might not miss his object.— I have heard that the heroes on the path of God will not distress the hearts of their enemies. How canst thou attain this dignified station who art at strife and warfare with thy friends?

The loving kindness of the righteous, whether before your face or behind your back, is not such that they will censure you when absent, and offer to die for you when present.— Face to face meek as a lamb, behind your back like a man-devouring wolf. Whoever brings you, and sums up the faults of others, will doubtless expose your defects to them.

V

Some traveling mendicants had agreed to club in a body and participate in the cares and comforts of society. I expressed a wish that I might be one of the party, but they refused to admit me. I said: "It is rare and inconsistent with the generous dispositions of dervishes to turn their faces from a good-fellowship with the poor, and to deny them its benefits, for on my part I feel such a zeal and good-will, that in the service of the liberal I am likely to prove rather an active associate than a grievous load.

"Though not one of those who are mounted on the camels,
I will do my best, that I may carry their saddle-cloths."

One of them answered and said: "Be not offended at what you have heard, for some days back a thief joined us in the garb of a dervish, and strung himself upon the cord of our acquaintance.— How can people know what he is that wears that dress? The writer can alone tell the contents of the letter." In consequence of that reverence in which the dervish character is held, they did not think of his profligacy and admitted him into their society. The outward character of the holy is a patched cloak; this much is sufficient, that it has a threadbare hood. Be industrious in thy calling, and wear whatever dress thou choosest. Put a diadem on thy head, and bear a standard on thy shoulder. Holiness does not consist in a coarse frock. Let a *zahid,* or holy man, be truly pious, and he may dress in satin. Sanctity is not merely a change of dress; it is an abandonment of the world, its pomp and vanity. It requires a hero to wear a coat of mail, for what would it profit to dress an hermaphrodite, or coward, in a suit of armor?

In short we had one day traveled till dark, and at night composed ourselves for sleep under the wall of a castle. That graceless thief took up his neighbor's ewer, saying, "I am going to my ablutions"; and he was setting out for plunder. Behold a religious man, who threw a patched cloak over his shoulders; he made the covering of the Kaaba the housing of an ass. So soon as he got out of sight of the dervishes, he scaled a bastion of the fort and stole a casket. Before break of day that gloomy-minded robber had got a great way off, and left his innocent companions asleep. In the morning they were all carried into the citadel, and thrown into a dungeon. From that time we have declined any addition to our party, and kept apart to ourselves,

For there is safety in unity,
But danger in duality or a multitude.

When an individual of a sect committed an act of folly, the high and the low sank in their dignity. Dost thou not see that one ox in a pasturage will cast a slur upon all the oxen of the village?

I said: "Let there be thanksgiving to a Deity of majesty and glory that I am not forbid the benefits of dervishes, notwithstanding I am in appearance excluded from their society; and I am instructed by this narration, and others like me may profit by its moral during their remaining lives.—From one indiscreet person in an assembly a host of the prudent may get hurt. If they fill a cistern to the brim with rose-water, and let a dog fall into it, the whole will be contaminated."

VI

A *zahid* was the guest of a king. When he sat down at table he ate more sparingly from that than his appetite inclined him, and when he stood up at prayers he continued longer at them than it was his custom; that they might form a high opinion of his sanctity.—I fear, O Arab! that thou wilt not reach the Kaaba; for the road that thou art taking leads to Turkistan, or the region of infidels.

When he returned home he ordered the table to be spread that he might eat. His son was a youth of a shrewd understanding. He said: "O father, perhaps you ate little or nothing at the feast of the king?" He answered, "In his presence I ate scarce anything that could answer its purpose!" Then retorted the boy, "Repeat also your prayers, that nothing be omitted that can serve a purpose." Yes, thy virtues thou hast exposed in the palm of thy hand, thy vices thou hast hid under thy arm-pit. Take heed, O hypocrite, what thou wilt be able to purchase with this base money on the day of need or day of judgment.

VII

I remember that in my early youth I was overmuch religious and vigilant, and scrupulously pious and abstinent. One night I sat up in attendance on my father, on whom be God's mercy, never once closed my eyes during the whole night, and held the precious Koran open on my lap, while the company around us were fast asleep. I said to my father: "Not an individual of these will raise his head that he may perform his genuflections, or ritual of prayer; but they are all so sound asleep, that you might conclude they were dead." He replied: "O emanation of your father, you had also better have slept than that you should thus calumniate the failings of mankind.— The braggart can discern only his own precious person; he will draw the veil of conceit all around him. Were fortune to bestow upon him God's all-searching eye, he would find nobody weaker than himself."

X

On one occasion, at the metropolitan mosque of Balbuk, I was holding forth, by way of admonition to a congregation cold and dead at heart, and not to be moved from the materialism of this world into the paths of mysticism. I perceived that the spirit of my discourse was making no impression, nor were the sparks of my enthusiasm likely to strike fire into their humid wood. I grew weary of instructing brutes, and of holding up a mirror to an assembly of the blind; but the door of exposition was thrown open, and the chain of argument extended; and in explanation of this text in the Koran, "We are nearer to him (God) than the vein of his neck"— I had reached that passage of my sermon where I thus express myself: "Such a mistress as is closer to me in her affection than I am to myself, but this is marvelous that I am estranged from her. What shall I say, and to whom can I tell it, that she lies on my bosom and I am alienated from her."

The intoxicating spirit of this discourse ran into my head, and the dregs of the cup still rested in my hand, when a traveler, as passing by, entered the outer circle of the congregation, and its expiring undulation lit upon him. He sent forth such a groan that the others in sympathy with him joined in lamentation, and the rawest of the assembly bubbled in unison. I exclaimed, "Praise be to God! those far off are present in their knowledge, and those near by are distant from their ignorance. If the hearer has not the faculty of comprehending the sermon, expect not the vigor of genius in the preacher. Give a scope to the field of inclination, that the orator may have room to strike the ball of eloquence over it."

XI

One night in the desert of Mecca, from an excess of drowsiness, I had not a foot to enable me to proceed; and, laying my head on the earth, I gave myself up for lost, and desired the camel-driver to leave me to my fate.— How could the foot of the poor jaded pedestrian go on, now that the Bactrian dromedary got impatient of its burden? While the body of a fat man is getting lean, a lean man must fall the victim of a hardship.

The camel-driver replied: "O brother, holy Mecca is ahead, and the profane robber behind; if you come forward you escape, but if you stay here you die!" During the night journey of the caravan, and in the track of the desert, it is fascinating to doze under the acacia-thorn tree; but, on this indulgence, we must resign all thoughts of surviving it.

XII

I saw on the seashore a holy man who had been torn by a tiger, and could get no salve to heal his wound. For a length of time he suffered much pain, and was all along offering thanks to the Most High. They asked him, saying, "Why are you so grateful?" He answered, "God be praised that I am overtaken with misfortune and not with sin! Were that beloved friend, God, to give me over to death, take heed, and think not that I should be solicitous about life. I would ask, What hast thou seen amiss in thy poor servant that thy heart should take offense at me? for that could alone give me a moment's uneasiness."

XIII

Having some pressing occasion, a dervish stole a rug from the hut of a friend. The judge ordered that they should cut off his hand. The owner of the rug made intercession for him, saying, "I have forgiven him." The judge replied, "At your instance I can not relax the extreme sentence of the law." He said: "In what you ordered you spoke justly. Nevertheless, whoever steals a portion of any property dedicated to alms must not suffer the forfeiture of his hand, for

A religious mendicant is not the proprietor of anything;

and whatever appertains to dervishes is devoted to the necessitous." The judge withdrew his hand from punishing him, and by way of reprimand asked, "Had the world become so circumscribed that you could not commit a theft but in the dwelling of such a friend?" He answered, "Have you not heard what they have said, 'Sweep everything away from the houses of your friends, but knock not at the doors of your enemies.' When overwhelmed with calamity let not thy body pine in misery. Strip thy foes of their skins, and thy friends of their jackets."

XIV

A king said to a holy man, "Are you ever thinking of me?" "Yes," replied he, "at such times as I am forgetting God Almighty! He will wander all around whom God shall drive from his gate; and he will not let him go to another door whom he shall direct into his own."

XV

One of the righteous in a dream saw a king in paradise, and a *parsa,* or holy man, in hell. He questioned himself, saying, "What is the cause of the exaltation of this, and the degradation of that, for we have fancied their converse?" A voice came from above, answering, "This king is in heaven because of his affection for the holy, and that *parsa* is in hell because of his connection with the kingly."— What can a coarse frock, rosary, and patched cloak avail? Abstain from such evil works as may defile thee. There is no occasion to put a felt cowl upon thy head. Be a dervish in thy actions, and wear a Tartarian coronet.

XVI

A pedestrian, naked from head to foot, left Cufah with the caravan of pilgrims for Hijaz, or Mecca, and came along with us. I looked at and saw him destitute of every necessary for the journey; yet he was cheerfully pushing on, and bravely remarking: "I am neither mounted on a camel nor a mule under a burden. I am neither the lord of vassals nor the vassal of a lord. I think not of present sorrows or past vanities, but breathe the breath of ease and live the life of freedom!"

A gentleman mounted on a camel said to him, "O dervish, whither are you going? return, or you must perish miserably." He did not heed what he said, but entered the desert on foot and proceeded. On our reaching the palm plantation of Mahmud, fate overtook the rich man, and he died. The dervish went up to his bier and said, "I did not perish amidst hardship on foot, and you expired on a camel's back." A person sat all night weeping by the side of a sick friend. Next day he died, and the invalid recovered! — Yes! many a fleet horse perished by the way, and that lame ass reached the end of the journey. How many of the vigorous and hale did they put underground, and that wounded man recovered!

XX

They asked Lucman, the fabulist, "From whom did you learn manners?" He answered, "From the unmannerly, for I was careful to avoid whatever part of their behavior seemed to me bad." They will not speak a word in joke from which the wise can not derive instruction; let them read a hundred chapters of wisdom to a fool, and they will all seem but a jest to him.

XXI

They tell a story of an *abid,* who in the course of a night would eat ten *mans,* or pounds, of food, and in his devotions repeat the whole Koran before morning. A good and holy man heard this, and said, "Had he eaten half a loaf of bread, and gone to sleep, he would have done a more meritorious act." Keep thy inside unencumbered with victuals, that the light of good works may shine within thee; but thou art void of wisdom and knowledge, because thou art filled up to the nose with food.

XXII

The divine favor had placed the lamp of grace in the path of a wanderer in forbidden ways, till it directed him into the circle of the righteous, and the blessed society of dervishes, and their spiritual co-operation enabled him to convert his wicked propensities into praiseworthy deeds, and to restrain himself in sensual indulgences; yet were the tongues of calumniators questioning his sincerity, and saying, He retains his original habits, and there is no trusting to his piety and goodness.— By the means of repentance thou mayest get delivered from the wrath of God, but there is no escape from the slanderous tongue of man. He was unable to put up with the virulence of their remarks, and took his complaint to his ghostly father, saying, "I am much troubled by the tongues of mankind." The holy man wept, and answered, "How can you be sufficiently grateful for this blessing, that you are better than they represent you? — How often wilt thou call aloud, saying, The malignant and envious are calumniating wretched me, that they rise up to shed my blood, and that they sit down to devise me mischief. Be thou good thyself, and let people speak evil of thee; it is better than to be wicked, and that they should consider thee as good."— But, on the other hand, behold me, of whose perfectness all entertain the best opinion, while I am the mirror of imperfection.— Had I done what they have said, I should have been a pious and moral man.

Verily, I may conceal myself from the sight of my neighbor,
But God knows what is secret and what is open.

There is a shut door between me and mankind, that they may not pry into my sins; but what, O Omniscience! can a closed door avail against thee, who art equally informed of what is manifest or concealed?

XXIII

I lodged a complaint with one of our reverend Shaikhs, saying: "A certain person has borne testimony against my character on the score of lasciviousness." He answered, "Shame him by your continence.—Be thou virtuously disposed, that the detractor may not have it in his power to indulge his malignity. So long as the harp is in tune, how can it have its ear pulled (or suffer correction by being put in tune) by the minstrel?"

XXIV

They asked one of the Shaikhs of Sham, or Syria, saying: "What is the condition of the Sufi sect?" He answered, "Formerly they were in this world a fraternity dispersed in the flesh, but united in the spirit; but now they are a body well clothed carnally, and ragged in divine mystery." Whilst thy heart will be every moment wandering into a different place, in thy recluse state thou canst not see purity; but though thou possessest rank and wealth, lands and chattels, if thy heart be fixed on God, thou art a hermit.

XXV

On one occasion we had marched, I recollect, all the night along with the caravan, and halted toward morning on the skirts of the wilderness. One mystically distracted, who accompanied us on that journey, set up a loud lamentation at dawn, went a-wandering into the desert, and did not take a moment's rest. Next day I said to him, "What condition was that?" He replied, "I remarked the nightingales that they had come to carol in the groves, the pheasants to prattle on the mountains, the frogs to croak in the pools, and the wild beasts to roar in the forests, and thought with myself, saying, It can not be generous that all are awake in God's praise and I am wrapt up in the sleep of forgetfulness!—Last night a bird was caroling toward the morning; it stole my patience and reason, my fortitude and understanding. My lamentation had perhaps reached the ear of one of my dearly-beloved friends. He said, 'I did not believe that the singing of a bird could so distract thee!' I answered, This is not the duty of the human species, that the birds are singing God's praise and that I am silent."

XXVI

Once, on a pilgrimage to Hijaz, I was the fellow-traveler of some piously disposed young men, and on a footing of familiarity and intimacy with them. From time to time we were humming a tune and chanting a spiritual hymn, and an *abid,* who bore us company, kept disparaging the morals of the dervishes, and was callous to their sufferings, till we reached the palm plantation of the tribe of Hulal, when a boy of a tawny complexion issued from the Arab horde and sung such a plaintive melody as would arrest the bird in its flight through the air. I remarked the *abid's* camel that it kicked up and pranced, and, throwing the *abid,* danced into the wilderness. I said: "O reverend Shaikh! that spiritual strain threw a brute into an ecstasy, and it is not in like manner working a change in you! — Knowest thou what that nightingale of the dawn whispered to me? What sort of man art thou, indeed, who art ignorant of love? — The camel is in an ecstacy of delight from the Arab's song. If thou hast no taste to relish this thou art a cross-grained brute.— Now that the camel is elated with rapture and delight, if a man is insensible to these he is an ass.

The zephyr, gliding through the verdure on the earth,
Shakes the twig of the ban-tree, but moves not the solid rock.

Whatever thou beholdest is loud in extolling him. That heart which has an ear is full of the divine mystery. It is not the nightingale that alone serenades his rose; for every thorn on the rose-bush is a tongue in his or God's praise!"

XXVII

A king had reached the end of his days and had no heir to succeed him. He made his will, stating, "You will place the crown of sovereignty upon the head of whatever person first enters the city gate in the morning, and commit the kingdom to his charge." It happened that the first man that presented himself at the city gate was a beggar, who had passed his whole life in scraping broken meat and in patching rags.

The ministers of State and nobles of the court fulfilled the conditions of the king's will, and laid the keys of the treasury and citadel at his feet.

For a time the dervish governed the kingdom, till some of the chiefs of the empire swerved from their allegiance, and the princes of the territories on every side rose in opposition to him, and levied armies for the contest. In short, his troops and subjects were routed and subdued, and several of his provinces taken from him.

The dervish was hurt to the soul at these events, when one of his old friends, who had been the companion of his state of poverty, returned from a journey and found him in such dignity. He exclaimed: "Thanksgiving be to a Deity of majesty and glory that lofty fortune succored you and prosperity was your guide, till roses issued from your thorns and the thorns were extracted from your feet, and till you arrived at this elevated rank!

Along with hardship there is ease; or, to sorrow succeeds joy.

The plant is at one season in flower and at another withered; the tree is at one time naked and at another clothed with leaves." He said: "O, my dear friend, offer me condolence, for here is no place for congratulation. When you last saw me I had to think of getting a crumb of bread; now I have the cares of a whole kingdom on my head." If the world be adverse, we are the victims of pain; if prosperous, the fettered slaves of affection for it. Amidst this life no calamity is more afflicting than that, whether fortunate or not, the mind is equally disquieted. If thou covetest riches, ask not but for contentment, which is an immense treasure. Should a rich man throw money into thy lap, take heed, and do not look upon it as a benefit; for I have often heard from the great and good that the patience of the poor is more meritorious than the gift of the rich. Were King Bahram Ghor to distribute a whole roasted elk, it would not be equal to the gift of a locust's leg from an ant."

XXVIII

A person had a friend who was holding the office of king's

divan, or prime minister, and it happened that he had not seen him for some time. Somebody remarked, saying, "It is some time since you saw such a gentleman." He answered, "I am no ways anxious about seeing him." One of the divan's people chanced to be present. He asked, "What has happened amiss that you should dislike to visit him?" He replied, "There is no dislike; but my friend, the divan, can be seen at a time when he is out of office, and my idle intrusion might not come amiss." Amidst the State patronage and authority of office they might take umbrage at their acquaintance; but on the day of vexation and loss of place they would impart their mental disquietudes to their friends.

XXXV

They asked a profoundly learned man, saying, "What is your opinion of consecrated bread, or almstaking?" He answered, "If with the view of composing their minds, and promoting their devotions, it is lawful to take it; but if monks collect for the sake of an endowment, it is forbidden. Good and holy men have received the bread of consecration for the sake of religious retirement; and are not recluses, that they may receive such bread."

XXXVI

A dervish came to put up at a place where the master of the house was a gentleman of an hospitable disposition. He had as his guests an assembly of learned and witty men, each of whom was repeating such a jest, or anecdote, as is usual with the facetious. Having traveled across a desert, the dervish was much fatigued, and well-nigh famished. One of the company observed, in the way of pleasantry, "You must also repeat something." The dervish answered, "I am not, like the others, overstocked with learning and wit, nor am I much read in books; and you must be satisfied with my reciting one distich." One and all eagerly cried, "Let us hear it." He said, "Hungry as I am, I sit by a table spread with food, like a bachelor at the entrance of a bath full of women!"

They applauded what he said, and ordered the tray to be

placed before him. The lord of the feast said, "Stay your appetite, my friend! till my handmaids can prepare for you some forced meat." He raised his head from the tray, and answered, "Say there is no need for forced meat on my tray, for a crust of plain bread is sufficient for one baked as I have been in the desert."

XXXVII

A disciple complained to his ghostly father, saying, "What can I do, for I am much annoyed by the people, who are interrupting me with their frequent visits, and break in upon my precious hours with their impertinent intrusions." He replied, "To such of them as are poor lend money, and from such as are rich ask some in loan; and neither of them will trouble you again." Let a beggar be the harbinger of an army of Islam, or the orthodox, and the infidel will fly his importunity as far as the wall of China.

XXXIX

A drunken fellow had lain down to sleep on the highway, and was quite overcome with the fumes of intoxication. An *abid* was passing close by, and looking at him with scorn. The youth raised his head, and said,

"Whenever they pass anything shameful they pass it with compassion.
Whenever thou beholdest a sinner, hide and bear with his transgressions:
Thou, who art aware of them, why not overlook my sins with pity?

Turn not away, O reverend sir! from a sinner; but look upon him with compassion. Though in my actions I am not a hero, do thou pass by as the heroic would pass me."

XL

A gang of dissolute vagabonds broke in upon a dervish, used opprobrious language, and beat and ill-used him. In his helplessness he carried his complaint before his ghostly father, and said, "Thus it has befallen me." He replied:

"O my son! the patched cloak of dervishes is the garment of resignation; whosoever wears this garb, and can not bear with disappointment, is a hypocrite, and to him our cloth is forbidden.— A vast and deep river is not rendered turbid by throwing into it a stone. That religious man who can be vexed at an injury is as yet a shallow brook.— If thou art subjected to trouble, bear with it; for by forgiveness thou art purified from sin. Seeing, O brother! that we are ultimately to become dust, be humble as the dust, before thou molderest into dust."

XLI

Hear what occurred once at Bagdad in a dispute that took place between a roll-up curtain and standard. Covered with the road-dust, and jaded with a march, the standard, in reproach, observed to the curtain: "Thou and I are gentlemen in livery; we are fellow-servants at the court of his majesty. I never enjoy a moment's relief from duty; early and late I am equally marching. Thou hast never experienced any peril or a siege, the heavy sand of the desert or dust of a whirlwind; my foot is most forward in any enterprise. Then why art thou my superior in dignity? Thou art cared for by youths with faces splendid as the moon, and handled by damsels scenting like jasmine; while I am fallen into the hands of raw recruits, am rolled upon our march, and turned upside down." The curtain answered: "I lay my head humble at the threshold, and hold it not up like thine, flaring in the face of heaven! Whoever is thus vainly rearing his crest exalts himself only to be humbled."

XLII

A good and holy man saw a huge and strong fellow, who, having got much enraged, was storming with passion and foaming at the mouth. He asked, "What has happened to this man?" Somebody answered, "Such a one has given him bad names!" He said, "This paltry wretch is able to carry a thousand-weight of stone, and can not bear with one light word! Cease to boast of thy strong arm and pretended manhood, infirm as thou art in mind, and mean in spirit. What difference is there between such a man and a woman? Though thou art strong of arm, let thy mouth utter sweet words; it is no proof of courage to thrust thy fist into another man's face.— Though thou art able to tear the scalp off an elephant, if deficient in humanity, thou art no hero. The sons of Adam are formed from dust; if not humble as the dust, they fall short of being men."

XLIV

A facetious old gentleman of Bagdad gave his daughter in marriage to a shoemaker. The flint-hearted fellow bit so deeply into the damsel's lip that the blood trickled from the wound. Next morning the father found her in this plight; he went up to his son-in-law, and asked him, saying: "Low-born wretch! what sort of teeth are these that thou shouldst chew her lips as if they were a piece of leather? I speak not in play what I have to say. Lay jesting aside, and take with her thy legal enjoyment.— When once a vicious disposition has taken root in the habit, the hand of death can only eradicate it."

XLV

A doctor of laws had a daughter preciously ugly, and she had reached the age of womanhood; but, notwithstanding her dowry and fortune, nobody seemed inclined to ask her in marriage.— Damask or brocade but add to her deformity when put upon a bride void of symmetry.

In short, they were under the necessity of uniting her in the bonds of wedlock to a blind man. They add, that soon after there arrived from Sirandip, or Ceylon, a physician that could restore sight to the blind. They spoke to the law doctor, saying, "Why do you not get him to prescribe for your son-in-law?" He answered: "Because I am afraid he may recover his sight, and repudiate my daughter; for—'the husband of an ugly woman should be blind.'"

XLVIII

They asked a wise man which was preferable, munificence

or courage? He answered, "Whoever has munificence has no need of courage." On the tombstone of Bahram-gor was inscribed: "The hand of liberality is stronger than the arm of power.— Hatim Tayi remains not, yet will his exalted name live renowned for generosity to all eternity. Distribute the tithe of thy wealth in alms, for the more the gardener prunes his vine the more he adds to his crop of grapes."

Chapter III

ON THE PRECIOUSNESS OF CONTENTMENT

I

A mendicant from the west of Africa had taken his station amidst a group of shopkeepers at Aleppo, and was saying: "O lords of plenty! had ye a just sense of equity, and we of contentment, all manner of importunity would cease in this world!" O contentment! do thou make me rich, for without thee there is no wealth. The treasure of patience was the choice of Lokman. Whoever has no patience has no wisdom.

II

There dwelt in Egypt two youths of noble birth, one of whom applied himself to study knowledge, and the other to accumulate wealth. In process of time that became the wisest man of his age, and this King of Egypt. Then was the rich man casting an eye of scorn upon his philosophic brother, and saying, "I have reached a sovereignty, and you remain thus in a state of poverty." He replied: "O brother! I am all the more grateful for the bounty of a Most High God, whose name was glorified, that I have found the heritage of the prophets — namely, wisdom; and you have got the estate of Pharaoh and Haman — that is, the kingdom of Egypt. I am an emmet, that mankind shall tread under foot; not a hornet, that they shall complain of my sting. How can I sufficiently express my grateful sense of this blessing, that I possess not the means of injuring my fellow creatures?"

III

I heard of a dervish who was consuming in the flame of want, tacking patch after patch upon his ragged garment, and solacing his mind with this couplet: "I can rest content with a dry crust of bread and a coarse woolen frock, for the burden of my own exertion bears lighter than laying myself under obligation to another."— Somebody observed to him, "Why do you sit quiet, while a certain gentleman of this city is so nobly disposed and universally benevolent, that he has girt up his loins in the service of the religious independents, and seated himself by the door of their hearts? Were he apprised of your condition, he would esteem himself obliged, and be happy in the opportunity of relieving it." He said: "Be silent; for it is better to die of want than to expose our necessities before another, as they have remarked: 'Patching a tattered cloak and the consequent treasure of content, is more commendable than petitioning the great for every new garment.'" By my troth, I swear it were equal to the torments of hell to enter into paradise through the interest of a neighbor.

IV

One of the Persian kings sent a skilful physician to attend Mohammed Mustafa, on whom be salutation. He remained some years in the territory of the Arabs; but nobody went to try his skill, or asked him for any medicine. One day he presented himself before the blessed prince of prophets, and complained, saying, "The king had sent me to dispense medicine to your companions; but, till this moment, nobody has been so good as to enable me to practise any skill that this your servant may possess." The blessed messenger of God was pleased to answer, saying, "It is a rule with this tribe never to eat till hard pressed by hunger, and to discontinue their repast while they have yet an appetite." The physician said, "This accounts for their health." Then he kissed the earth of respect and took his leave. The physician will then begin to inculcate temperance, or to extend the finger of indulgence, when from silence his patient might suffer by excess, or his life be endangered by abstinence: of course, the skill of the physician is advice, and the patient's regimen and diet yield the fruits of health!

V

A certain person would be making vows of abstinence and breaking them. At last a reverend gentleman observed to him, "So I understand that you make a practise of eating to excess; and that any restraint on your appetite, namely, this vow, is weaker than a hair, and this voraciousness, as you indulge it, would break an iron chain; but the day must come when it will destroy you." A man was rearing the whelp of a wolf; when full grown it tore its patron and master.

VI

In the annals of Ardishir Babagan it is recorded that he asked an Arabian physician, saying, "What quantity of food ought to be eaten daily?" He replied, "A hundred dirams' weight were sufficient." The king said, "What strength can a man derive from so small a quantity?" The physician replied: "So much can support you; but in whatever you exceed that you must support it.— Eating is for the purpose of living, and speaking in praise of God; but thou believest that we live only to eat."

VII

Two dervishes of Khorassan were fellow-companions on a journey. One was so spare and moderate that he would break his fast only every other night, and the other so robust and intemperate that he ate three meals a day. It happened that they were taken up at the gate of a city on suspicion of being spies, and both together put into a place, the entrance of which was built up with mud. After a fortnight it was discovered that they were innocent, when, on breaking open the door, they found the strong man dead, and the weak one alive and well. They were astonished at this circumstance. A wise man said, "The contrary of this had been strange, for this one was a voracious eater, and not having strength to support a want of food, perished; and that other was abstemious, and being patient, according to his habitual practise, survived it.— When a person is habitually temperate, and a hardship shall cross him, he will get over it with ease; but if he has pampered his body and lived in luxury, and shall get into straitened circumstances, he must perish."

XI

In a battle with the Tartars, a gallant young man was grievously wounded. Somebody said to him, "A certain merchant has a stock of the mummy antidote; if you would ask him, he might perhaps accommodate you with a portion of it." They say that merchant was so notorious for his stinginess, that —"If, in the place of his loaf of bread, the orb of the sun had been in his wallet, nobody would have seen daylight in the world till the day of judgment."

The spirited youth replied: "Were I to ask him for this antidote, he might give it, or he might not; and if he did it might cure me, or it might not; at any rate, to ask such a man were itself a deadly poison!" Whatever thou wouldst ask of the mean, in obligation, might add to the body, but would take from the soul.— And philosophers have observed, that were the water of immortality, for example, to be sold at the price of the reputation, a wise man would not buy it, for an honorable death is preferable to a life of infamy.— Wert thou to eat colocynth from the hand of the kind-hearted, it would relish better than a sweetmeat from that of the crabbed.

XII

One of the learned had a large family and small means. He stated his case to a great man, who entertained a favorable opinion of his character. This one turned away from his solicitation, and viewed this prostitution of begging as discreditable with a gentleman of education. If soured by misfortune, present not thyself before a dear friend, for thou may'st also embitter his pleasure. When thou bringest forward a distress, do it with a cheerful and smiling face, for an openness of countenance can never retard business.— They have related that he rose a little in the pension, but sank much in the estimation of the great man. After some days, when he perceived this falling off in his affection, he said:

"Miserable is that supply of food which thou obtainest in the
hour of need;
The pot is put to boil, but my reputation is bubbled into vapor.

—He added to my means of subsistence, but took from my reputation; absolute starving were better than the disgrace of begging."

XIII

A dervish had a pressing call for money. Somebody told him a certain person is inconceivably rich; were he made aware of your want, he would somehow manage to accommodate it. He said, "I do not know him." The other answered, "I will introduce you"; and having taken his hand, he brought him to that person's dwelling. The dervish beheld a man with a hanging lip, and sitting in sullen discontent. He said nothing, and returned home. His friend asked, "What have you done?" He replied, "His gift I gave in exchange for his look: Lay not thy words before a man with a sour face, otherwise thou may'st be ruffled by his ill-nature. If thou tellest the sorrows of thy heart let it be to him in whose countenance thou may'st be assured of prompt consolation."

XVI

The Prophet Moses, on whom be peace, saw a dervish who had buried his body, in his want of clothes to cover it, in the sand. He said: "O Moses, put up a prayer, that the Most High God would bestow a subsistence upon me, for I am perishing in distress." The blessed Moses prayed accordingly, that God on high would succor him.

Some days afterward, as he was returning from a conference with God on Mount Sinai, he met that dervish in the hands of justice, and a mob following him. He asked: "What has befallen this man?" They answered: "He had drunk wine and got into a quarrel, and having killed somebody, they are now going to exact retaliation."— The God who set forth the seven climates of this world assigned to every creature its appropriate lot. Had that wretched cat been gifted with wings, she would not have left one sparrow's egg on the earth. It might happen that were a weak man to get the ability, he would rise and domineer over his weak brethren.

The blessed Moses acknowledged the wisdom of the Creator of the universe, and confessing his own presumption, repeated this verse of the Koran: "Were God to spread abroad his stores of subsistence to servants, verily they would rebel all over the earth": What happened, O vain man! that thou didst precipitate thyself into destruction? Would that the ant might not have the means of flying! — A mean person, when he has got rank and wealth, will bring a storm of blows upon his head. Was not this at last the adage of a philosopher, 'That ant is best disposed of that has no wings.'— The father is a man of much sweetness of disposition, but the son is full of heat and passions.— That Being, God, who would not make thee rich, must have known thy good better than thou couldst thyself know it.

XVII

I saw an Arab, who was standing amidst a circle of jewelers at Busrah, and saying: "On one occasion I had missed my way in the desert, and having no road-provision left, I had given myself up for lost, when all at once I found a bag of pearls. Never shall I forget that relish and delight, so long as I mistook them for parched wheat; nor that bitterness and disappointment, when I discovered that they were real pearls." In the mouth of the thirsty traveler, amidst parched deserts and moving sands, pearl, or mother-of-pearl, were equally distasteful. To a man without provision, and exhausted in the desert, a piece of stone or of gold, in his scrip, is all one.

XVIII

An Arab, suffering under all the extremity of thirst in the desert, was saying:

"Would to God that yet, before I perish, I could but for one day gratify my wish:
That a stream of water might dash against my knees, and I could fill my leathern flask or stomach with it."

In like manner a traveler had got bewildered in the great desert, and had neither provisions nor strength left, yet a few dirams remained with him in his scrip. He kept wandering about, but could not find the path, and sank under his fatigue. A party of travelers arrived where his body lay; they saw the dirams spread before him, and these verses written in the sand: "Were he possessed of all the gold of Jafier (a famous gold refiner), a man without food could not satisfy his appetite. To a wretched mendicant, parched in the desert, a boiled turnip would relish better than an ingot of virgin silver."

XIX

I had never complained of the vicissitudes of fortune, nor murmured at the ordinances of heaven, excepting on one occasion, that my feet were bare, and I had not wherewithal to shoe them. In this desponding state I entered the metropolitan mosque at Cufah, and there I beheld a man that had no feet. I offered up praise and thanksgiving for God's goodness to myself, and submitted with patience to my want of shoes.— In the eyes of one satiated with meat a roast fowl is less esteemed at his table than a salad; but to him who is stinted of food a boiled turnip will relish like a roast fowl.

XX

A king, attended by a select retinue, had, on a sporting excursion during the winter, got at a distance from any of his hunting-seats, and the evening was closing fast, when they espied from afar a peasant's cottage. The king said: "Let us repair thither for the night, that we may shelter ourselves from the inclemency of the weather." One of the courtiers replied: "It would not become the dignity of the sovereign to take refuge in the cottage of a low peasant; we can pitch a tent here and kindle a fire." The peasant saw what was passing; he came forward with what refreshments he had at hand, and, laying them before the king, kissed the earth of subserviency, and said: "The lofty dignity of the king would not be lowered by this condescension; but these gentlemen did not choose that the condition of a peasant should be exalted." The king was pleased with this speech; and they passed the night at his cottage. In the morning he bestowed an honorary dress and handsome largess upon him. I have heard that the peasant was resting his hand for some paces upon the king's stirrup, and saying: "The state and pomp of the sovereign suffered no degradation by his condescension in becoming a guest at the cottage of a peasant; but the corner of the peasant's cap rose to the level with the sun when the shadow of such a monarch as thou art fell upon his head."

XXI

They tell a story of an importunate mendicant who had amassed much riches. A certain king said: "It seems that you possess immense wealth, and I have a business of some consequence in hand. If you will assist me with a little of it, by way of a loan, when the public revenue is realized I will repay it and thank you to the bargain." He replied: "O sire, it would ill become the sublime majesty of the sovereign of the universe to soil the hand of lofty enterprise with the property of such a mendicant as I am, which I have scraped together grain by grain." He said: "There is no occasion to vex yourself, for I mean it for the Tartars, as impurities are suiting for the impure:

"They said, 'The compost of a dung-hill is unclean.'
We replied, 'That with it we will fill up the chinks of a necessary.'"

"If the water of a Christian's well is defiled, and we wash a Jew's corpse in it, there is no sin." I have heard that he disobeyed the royal command, questioned its justice, and resisted it with insolence. The king ordered that the exchequer stipulations should be put in force with rigidness and violence. When a business can not be settled with fair words, we must of necessity make use of foul. When a man will not contribute of his own free will, if another enforces him he meets his desert.

XXII

I knew a merchant who had a hundred and fifty camels of burden and forty bondsmen and servants in his train. One night he entertained me at his lodgings in the island of Keish, in the Persian Gulf, and continued for the whole night talking idly, and saying: "Such a store of goods I have in Turkestan, and such an assortment of merchandise in Hindustan; this is the mortgage-deed of a certain estate, and this the security-bond of a certain individual's concern." Then he would say: "I have a mind to visit Alexandria, the air of which is salubrious; but that can not be, for the Mediterranean Sea is boisterous. O Sadi! I have one more journey in view, and, that once accomplished, I will pass my remaining life in retirement and leave off trade." I asked: "What journey is that?" He replied: "I will carry the sulphur of Persia to Chin, where, I have heard, it will fetch a high price; thence I will take China porcelain to Greece; the brocade of Greece or Venice I will carry to India; and Indian steel I will bring to Aleppo; the glassware of Aleppo I will take to Yamin; and with the bardimani, or striped stuffs, of Yamin I will return to Persia. After that I will give up foreign commerce and settle myself in a warehouse." He went on in this melancholy strain till he was quite exhausted with speaking. He said: "O Sadi! do you too relate what you have seen and heard." I replied: "Hast thou not heard that in the desert of Ghor as the body of a chief merchant fell exhausted from his camel, he said, 'Either contentment or the dust of the grave will fill the stingy eye of the worldly minded.'"

XXIV

A weak fisherman got a strong fish into his net, but not having the power of mastering it, the fish got the better of him, and, dragging the net from his hand, escaped.— A bondsman went that he might take water from the brook; the brook came to rise and carried off the bondsman. On most occasions the net would bring out the fish; on this occasion the fish escaped, and took away the net. The other fishermen expressed their vexation, and reproached him, saying, "Such a fish came into your net, and you were not able to master it." He replied: "Alas! my brethren, what could be done? It was not my day of fortune, and the fish had in this way another day left it. And they have said: 'Unless it be his lot, the fisherman can not catch a fish in the Tigris; and, except it be its fate, the fish will not die on the dry shore.'"

XXV

A person without hands or feet killed a milleped. A good and holy man passed by him at the time, and said: "Glory be to God! notwithstanding the thousand feet he had when his destiny overtook him, he was unable to escape from one destitute of hand or foot."— When the life-plundering foe comes up behind, fate arrests the speed of the swift-going warrior. At the moment when the enemy might approach step by step it were useless to bend the *kayani,* or Parthian bow.

XXVI

I met a fat blockhead decked in rich apparel, and mounted on an Arab horse, with a turban of fine Egyptian linen on his head. A person said: "O Sadi, how comes it that you see these garments of the learned on this ignorant beast?" I replied: "It is a vile epistle which has been written in golden letters:

"'Verily this ass, with the resemblance of a man,
Has the carcass of a calf, and the voice or bleating of a calf.'"

Thou canst not say that this brute appears like a man, unless in his garments, turban, and outward form. Examine into all the ways and means of his existence, and thou shalt find nothing lawful but the shedding of his blood: though a man of noble birth be reduced to poverty, imagine not that his lofty dignity can be lowered; and though he may secure his silver threshold with a hasp of gold, conclude not that a Jew can be thereby ennobled."

XXVII

A thief said to a mendicant: "Are you not ashamed when you hold forth your hand to every mean fellow for a barley-corn of silver?" He replied: "It is better to hold forth the hand for one grain of silver than to have it cut off for one and a half dang."

XXIX

I saw a dervish who had withdrawn into a cave, shut the door of communication between the world and himself, and with his lofty and independent eye viewed emperors and kings without awe or reverence.— Whoever opens to himself the door of mendicity must continue a beggar till the day of his death. Put covetousness aside, and be independent as a prince; the neck of contentment can raise its head erect.

One of the sovereigns of those parts sent a message to him, stating: "So far I can rely on the generous disposition of his reverence, that he will one day favor me by partaking of my bread and salt, by becoming my guest." The shaikh, or holy man, consented; for the acceptance of such an invitation accorded with the sunnat, or law and tradition of the prophet. Next day the king went to apologize for the trouble he had caused him. The *abid* rose from his place, took the king in his arms, showed him much kindness, and was full of his compliments. After he was gone, one of the shaikh's companions asked him, saying: "Was not such condescending kindness as you this day showed the king contrary to what is usual; what does this mean?" He answered: "Have you not heard what they have said: 'It is proper to stand up and administer to him whom thou hast seated on thy carpet, or made thy guest.'"

He could so manage that, during his whole life, his ear should not indulge in the music of the tabor, cymbal, and pipe. He could restrain his eyes from enjoying the garden, and gratify his sense of smell without the rose or narcissus. Though he had not a pillow stuffed with down, he could compose himself to rest with a stone under his head; though he had no heart-solacer as the partner of his bed, he could hug himself to sleep with his arms across his breast. If he could not ride an ambling nag, he was content to take his walk on foot; only this grumbling and vile belly he could not keep under, without stuffing it with food.

Chapter IV

ON THE BENEFIT OF BEING SILENT

I

I spoke to one of my friends, saying: "A prudent restraint on my words is on that account advisable, because in conversation there on most occasions occur good and bad; and the eyes of rivals only note what is bad. He replied: "O brother! that is our best rival who does not, or will not, see our good!

The malignant brotherhood pass not by the virtuous man
Without imputing to him what is infamous.

To the eye of enmity, virtue appears the ugliest blemish; it is a rose, O Sadi! which to the eyes of our rivals seems a thorn. The world-illuminating brilliancy of the fountain of the sun, in like manner, appears dim to the eye of the purblind mole."

II

A merchant happened to lose a thousand dinars. He said to his son: "It will be prudent not to mention this loss to anybody." The son answered: "O father, it is your orders, and I shall not mention it; but communicate the benefit so far, as what the policy may be in keeping it a secret." He said: "That I may not suffer two evils: one, the loss of my money; another, the reproach of my neighbor.— Impart not thy grievances to rivals, for they are glad at heart, while praying, God preserve us; or

"'There is neither strength nor power, unless it be from God!'"

III

A sensible youth made vast progress in the arts and sciences, and was of a docile disposition; but however much he frequented the societies of the learned, they never could get him to utter a word. On one occasion his father said: "O my son, why do not you also say what you know on this subject?" He replied: "I am afraid lest they question me upon what I know not, and put me to shame.— Hast thou not heard of a Sufi who was hammering some nails into the sole of his sandal. An officer of cavalry took him by the sleeve, saying, 'Come along, and shoe my horse.'— So long as thou art silent and quiet, nobody will meddle with thy business; but once thou divulgest it, be ready with thy proofs."

IV

A man, respectable for his learning, got into a discussion with an atheist; but, failing to convince him, he threw down his shield and fled. A person asked him, "With all your wisdom and address, learning and science, how came you not to controvert an infidel?" He replied: "My learning is the Koran, and the traditions and sayings of our holy fathers; but he puts no faith in the articles of our belief, and what good could it do to listen to his blasphemy?" To him whom thou canst not convince by revelation or tradition, the best answer is that thou shalt not answer him.

VI

They have esteemed Sahban Wabil as unrivaled in eloquence, insomuch that he could speak for a year before an assembly, and would not use the same word twice; or should he chance to repeat it, he would give it a different signification; and this is one of the special accomplishments of a courtier.— Though a speech be captivating and sweet, worthy of belief, and meriting applause, yet what thou hast once delivered thou must not repeat, for if they eat a sweetmeat once they find that enough.

VII

I overheard a sage, who was remarking: "Never has anybody acknowledged his own ignorance, excepting that person who, while another may be talking, and has not finished what he has to say, will begin speaking: "A speech, O wiseacre! has a beginning and an end; bring not one speech into the middle of another. A man of judgment, discretion, and prudence, delivers not his speech till he find an interval of silence."

VIII

Some of the courtiers of Sultan Mahmud asked Husan Maimandi, saying: "What did the king whisper to you to-day on a certain State affair?" He said: "You are also acquainted with it." They replied: "You are the prime minister; what the king tells you, he does not think proper to communicate to such as we are." He replied: "He communicates with me in the confidence that I will not divulge to anybody; then why do you ask me" A man of sense blabs not, whatever he may come to know; he should not make his own head the forfeit of the king's secret.

IX

I was hesitating about the purchase of a dwelling-house. A Jew said: "I am an old housekeeper in this street: ask the character of this house from me and buy it, for it has no fault." I replied: "True! only that you are its neighbor.— Any such house as has thee for its neighbor could scarce be worth ten dirams of silver; yet it should behoove us to hope that after thy death it may fetch a thousand."

X

A certain poet presented himself before the chief of a gang of robbers, and recited a *casidah,* or elegy, in his praise. He ordered that they should strip off his clothes, and thrust him from the village. The naked wretch was going away shivering in the cold, and the village dogs were barking at his heels. He stooped to pick up a stone, in order to shy at the dogs, but found the earth frost-bound, and was disappointed. He exclaimed: "What rogues these villagers are, for they let loose their dogs, and tie up their stones!" The chief robber saw and overheard him from a window. He smiled at his wit, and, calling him near, said: "O learned sir! ask me for a boon." He replied, "I ask for my own garments, if you will vouchsafe to give them.

I shall have enough of boons in your suffering me to depart.

Mankind expects charity from others; I expect no charity from thee, only do me no injury." The chief robber felt compassion for him. He ordered his clothes to be restored, and added to them a robe of fur and sum of money.

XIII

At a mosque in the city of Sanjar, the capital of Khorassan, a person was volunteering to chant forth the call to prayers with so discordant a note as to drive all that heard him away in disgust. The intendant of that mosque was a just and well-disposed gentleman, who was averse to giving offense to anybody. He said: "O generous youth, there belong to this mosque some *mowuzzins,* or criers, of long standing, to each of whom I allow a monthly stipend of five dinars; now I will give you ten to go elsewhere." To this he agreed, and took himself off. After a while he came to the nobleman, and said: "O my lord! you did me an injury when for ten dinars you prevailed upon me to quit this station, for where I went they offered me twenty to remove to another place, but I would not consent." The nobleman smiled and replied: "Take heed, and do not accept them, for they may be content to give you fifty! — No person can with a mattock scrape off the clay from the face of a hard rock in so grating a manner as thy harsh voice is harrowing up my soul."

XIV

A person with a harsh voice was reciting the Koran in a loud tone. A good and holy man went up to him, and asked: "What is your monthly stipend?" He answered, "Nothing." "Then," added he, "why give yourself so much trouble?" He said: "I am reading for the sake of God." The good and holy man replied: "For God's sake do not read: for if thou chantest the Koran after this manner, thou must cast a shade over the glory of Islamism or Mussulman orthodoxy."

Chapter V

ON LOVE AND YOUTH

I

They asked Husan Maimandi: "How comes it that Sultan Mahmud, who has so many handsome bondswomen, each of whom is the wonder of the world and most select of the age, entertains not such fondness and affection for any of them as he does for Ayaz, who can boast of no superiority of charms?" He replied: "Whatever makes an impression on the heart seems lovely in the eye. That person of whom the sultan makes choice must be altogether good, though a compendium of vice; but where he is estranged from the favor of the king none of the household will think of courting him." Were a person to view it with a fastidious eye, the form of a Joseph might seem a deformity; but let him look with desire on a demon, and he will appear like an angel and cherub.

III

I saw a *parsa,* or holy man, so enamored of a lovely person that he had neither fortitude to bear with, nor resolution to declare, his passion; and, however much he was the object of remark and censure, he would not forego this infatuation, and was saying: "I quit not my hold on the skirt of thy garment, though thou may'st verily smite me with a sharp sword. Besides thee I have neither asylum nor defense; if I am to flee, I must take refuge with thee."

On one occasion I reproached him, and said: "What is become of your precious reason, that a vile passion should thus master you?" He made a short pause, and replied: "Wherever the king of love came, he left no room for the strong arm of chastity. How can that wretch live undefiled who has fallen in a quagmire up to the neck?"

IV

A certain person had lost his heart and abandoned himself to despair. The object of his desire was not such a dainty that he could gratify his palate with it, or a bird that he could lure it into his net, but a frightful precipice and overwhelming whirlpool.— When thy gold attracts not the charmer's eye, dust or gold is of equal value with thee.

His friends admonished him, saying: "Put aside this vain fancy, for multitudes are in the durance and chains of this same passion which you are cherishing." He sighed aloud, and replied: "Say to my friends, Do not admonish me, for my eye is fixed on the wish of her. With strength of wrist and power of shoulders warriors overwhelm their antagonists and charmers their lovers." Nor can it be consistent with the condition of love that any thought of life should divert the heart from affection for its mistress.— Thou, who art the slave of thine own precious self, playest false in the affairs of love. If thou canst not make good a passage to thy mistress, it is the duty of a lover to perish in the attempt.— I persist when policy is no longer left me, though the enemy may cover me all over with the wounds of swords and arrows. If I can reach her I will seize her sleeve, or at all events proceed and die at her threshold.

His kindred, whose business it was to watch over his concerns, and to pity his misfortunes, gave him advice, and put upon him restraints, but all to no good purpose.— The physician is, alas! prescribing bitter-aloes, and his depraved appetite is craving sweetmeats! — heardest thou what a charmer was saying in a whisper to one who had lost his heart to her: "So long as thou maintainest thine own dignity, of what value can my dignity appear in thine eye?"

They informed the princess who was the object of his infatuation, saying: "A youth of an amiable disposition and sweet flow of tongue is frequent in his attendance at the top of this plain; and we hear him delivering brilliant speeches and wonderful sallies of wit; it would seem that he has a mystery in his head and a flame in his heart, for he appears to be distractedly in love." The princess was aware that she had become the object of his attachment, and that this whirlwind of calamity was raised by himself, and spurred her horse toward him. Now that the youth saw that it was the princess' intention to approach him, he wept, and said: "That personage who inflicted upon me a mortal wound again presented herself before me; perhaps she took compassion upon her own victim." However, kindly she spoke, and asked, saying: "Who are you, and whence come you? what is your name, and what your calling?" the youth was so entirely overwhelmed in the ocean of love and passion that he absolutely could not utter a word: "Couldst thou in fact repeat the seven Saba, or whole Koran by heart, if distracted with love, thou wouldst forget the alphabet?"—the princess continued: "Why do you not answer me? for I too am one of the sect of dervishes, nay, I am their most devoted slave." On the strength of this sympathizing encouragement of his beloved, the youth raised his head amidst the buffeting waves of tempestuous passion, and answered: "It is strange that with thee present I should remain in existence; that after thou camest to talk, I should have speech left me."— This he said, and, uttering a loud groan, surrendered his soul up to God.— No wonder if he died by the door of his beloved's tent; the wonder was, if alive, how he could have brought his life back in safety.

V

A boy at school possessed much loveliness of person and sweetness of conversation; and the master, from the frailty of human nature, was enamored of his blooming skin. Like his other scholars, he would not admonish and correct him, but when he found him in a corner he would whisper in his ear: "I am not, O celestial creature! so occupied with thee, that I am harboring in my mind a thought of myself. Were I to perceive an arrow coming right into it, I could not shut my eye from contemplating thee."

On one occasion the boy said: "In like manner, as you inspect my duties, also animadvert on my tendency to vice, in order that if you discern any immorality in my behavior, which has met my own approbation, you can warn me against it, that I may correct it." He replied: "O my child! propose this task to somebody else; for the light in which I view you reflects nothing but virtue." That malignant eye, let it be plucked out in whose sight his virtue can seem vice. Hadst thou but one perfection and seventy faults, the lover could discern only that one perfection.

VII

A person who had not seen his friend for a length of time said to him: "Where were you? for I have been very solicitous about you." He replied, "It is better to be sought after than loathed." Thou hast come late, O intoxicating idol! I shall not in a hurry quit my hold on thy skirt: that mistress whom they see but seldom is at last more desired than she is whom they are cloyed with seeing.

The charmer that can bring companions along with her has come to quarrel; for she can not be void of jealousy and discontent:

Whenever thou comest to visit me attended with comrades or
rivals,
Though thou comest in peace, yet thy object is hostile.

For one single moment that my mistress associated with a rival, it went well-nigh to slay me with jealousy. Smiling, she replied: "O Sadi! I am the torch of the assembly; what is it to me if the moth consume itself?"

VIII

In former times, I recollect, a friend and I were associating together like two kernels within one almond shell. I happened unexpectedly to go on a journey. After some time, when I was returned, he began to chide me, saying: "During this long interval you never sent me a messenger." I replied: "It vexed me to think that the eyes of a courier should be enlightened by your countenance, whilst I was debarred that happiness.— Tell my old charmer not to impose a vow upon me with her tongue; for I would not repent, were she to attempt it with a sword. Envy stings me to the quick, lest another should be satiated with beholding thee, till I recollect myself, and say: Nobody can have a satiety of that!"

IX

I saw a learned gentleman the captive of attachment for a certain person, and the victim of his reproach; and he would suffer much violence, and bear it with great patience. On one occasion I said, by way of admonition: "I know that in your attachment for this person you have no bad object, and that this friendship rests not on any criminal design; yet, under this interpretation, it accords not with the dignity of the learned to expose yourself to calumny, and put up with the rudeness of the rabble." He replied: "O my friend, withdraw the hand of reproach from the skirt of my fatality, for I have frequently reflected on this advice which you offer me, and find it easier to suffer contumely on his account than to forego his company; and philosophers have said: 'It is less arduous to persist in the labor of courting than to restrain the eye from contemplating a beloved object.'— Whoever devotes his heart to a soul deluder puts his beard of reputation into the hands of another. That person, without whom thou canst not exist, if he do thee a violence, thou must bear it. The antelope, that is led by a string, can not bound from this side to that. One day I asked a compact of my mistress; how often have I since that day craved her forgiveness! A lover exacts not terms of his charmer; I relinquished my heart to whatever she desired me, whether to call me up to her with kindness, or drive me from her with harshness she knows best, or it is her pleasure."

X

In my early youth such an event (as you know) will come to pass. I held a mystery and intercourse with a young person, because he had a pipe of exquisite melody, and a form silver bright as the full moon.—"He is sipping the fountain of immortality, who may taste the down of his cheek; and he is eating a sweetmeat, who can fancy the sugar of his lips."

It happened that something in his behavior having displeased me, I withdrew the skirt of communication, and removed the seal of my affection from him, and said: "Go, and take what course best suits thee; thou regardest not my counsel, follow thine own." I overheard him as he was going, and saying: "If the bat does not relish the company of the sun, the all-current brilliancy of that luminary can suffer no diminution." He so expressed himself and departed, and his vagabond condition much distressed me:

The opportunity of enjoyment was lost,
And a man is insensible to the relish of prosperity till he has tasted adversity:

return and slay me, for to die before thy face were far more pleasant than to survive in thy absence.

But, thanksgiving and praise to the Almighty, he did not return till after some interval, when that melodious pipe of David was cracked, and that handsome form of Joseph in its wane; when that apple his chin was overgrown with hair, like a quince, and the all-current luster of his charms tarnished. He expected me to fold him in my arms; but I took myself aside and said: "When the down of loveliness flourished on thy cheek, thou drovest the lord of thy attractions from thy sight; now thou hast come to court his peace when thy face is thick set with *fathahs* and *zammahs*, or the bristles of a beard.— The verdant foliage of thy spring is turned yellow; place not thy kettle on my grate, for its fire is cooled. How long wilt thou display this pomp and vanity; hopest thou to regain thy former dominion? Make thy court to such as desire thee, sport thy airs on such as will hire thee.— The verdure of the garden, they have told us, is charming; that person (Sadi) knows it who is relating that story; or, in other words, that the fresh-shooting down on their charmers' cheeks is what the hearts of their admirers chiefly covet.— Thy garden is like a bed of chives: the more thou croppest it, the more it will shoot.— Last year thou didst depart smooth as an antelope, to-day thou art returned bearded like a pard. Sadi admires the fresh-shooting down, not when each hair is stiff as a packing-needle.— Whether thou hast patience with thy beard or weed it from thy face, this happy season of youth must come to a conclusion. Had I the same command of life as thou hast of beard, it should not escape me till doomsday." I asked him and said: "What has become of the beauty of thy countenance, that a beard has sprung up round the orb of the moon?" He answered: "I know not what has befallen my face, unless it has put on black to mourn its departed charms."

XII

They shut up a parrot in the same cage with a crow. The parrot was affronted at his ugly look, and said: "What an odious visage is this, a hideous figure; what an accursed appearance, and ungracious demeanor!

Would to God, O raven of the desert!
We were wide apart as the east is from the west:

The serenity of his peaceful day would change into the gloom of night, who on issuing forth in the morning might cross thy aspect. An ill-conditioned wretch like thyself should be thy companion; but where could we find such another in the world?"

But what is more strange, the crow was also out of all patience, and vexed to the soul at the society of the parrot. Bewailing his misfortune, he was railing at the revolutions of the skies; and, wringing the hands of chagrin, was lamenting his condition, and saying: "What an unpropitious fate is this; what ill-luck, and untoward fortune! Could they any way suit the dignity of me, who would in my day strut with my fellow-crows along the wall of a garden.— It were durance sufficient for a good and holy man that he should be made the companion of the wicked.— What sin have I committed that my stars in retribution of it have linked me in the chain of companionship, and immured me in the dungeon of calamity, with a conceited blockhead, and good-for-nothing babbler? — Nobody will approach the foot of a wall on which they have painted thy portrait; wert thou to get a residence in paradise, others would go in preference to hell."

I have introduced this parable to show that however much learned men despise the ignorant, these are a hundredfold more scornful of the learned.—A *zahid,* or holy man, fell in company with some wandering minstrels. One of them, a charmer of Balkh, said to him: "If thou art displeased with us, do not look sour, for thou art already sufficiently offensive. — An assemblage is formed of roses and tulips, and thou art stuck up amidst them like a withered stalk; like an opposing storm, and a chilling winter blast; like a ball of snow, or lump of ice."

XIII

I had an associate, who was for years the companion of my travels, partook of the same bread and salt, and enjoyed the many rights of a confirmed friendship. At last, on some trifling advantage, he gave me cause of umbrage, and our intimacy ceased. And notwithstanding all this, there was a hankering of good-will on both sides; in consequence of which I heard that he was one day reciting in a certain assembly these two couplets of my writings:

"When my idol, or mistress, is approaching me with her tantalizing smiles,
She is sprinkling more salt upon my smarting sores.
How fortunate were the tips of her ringlets to come into my hand,
Like the sleeve of the generous in the hands of dervishes."

This society of his friends bore testimony, and gave applause, not to the beauty of this sentiment, but to the liberality of his own disposition in quoting it; while he had himself been extravagant in his encomiums, regretted the demise of our former attachment, and confessed how much he was to blame. I was made aware that he too was desirous of a reconciliation; and, having sent him these couplets, made my peace.—"Was there not a treaty of good faith between us, and didst not thou commence hostilities, and violate the compact? I relinquished all manner of society, and plighted my heart to thee; for I did not suspect that thou wouldst have so readily changed. If it still be thy wish to renew our peace, return, and be more dear to me than ever."

XIV

A man had a beautiful wife, who died; but the mother, a decrepit old dotard, remained a fixture in his house, because of the dowry. He was teased to death by her company; but, from the circumstance of the dowry, he had no remedy. In the meantime some of his friends having come to comfort him, one of them asked: "How is it with you, since the loss of that dear friend?" He answered: "The absence of my wife is not so intolerable as the presence of her mother.— They plucked the rose, and left me the thorn; they plundered the treasure, and let the snake remain. To have one eye pierced with a spear were more tolerable than to see the face of an enemy. It were better to break with a thousand friends than to put up with one rival."

XV

In my youth I recollect I was passing through a street, and caught a glimpse of a moon-like charmer during the dog-days, when their heat was drying up the moisture of the mouth, and the samum, or desert hot-wind, melting the marrow of the bones. From the weakness of human nature I was unable to withstand the darting rays of a noon-tide sun, and took refuge under the shadow of a wall, hopeful that somebody would relieve me from the oppressive heat of summer, and quench the fire of my thirst with a draught of water. All at once I beheld a luminary in the shadowed portico of a mansion, so splendid an object that the tongue of eloquence falls short in summing up its loveliness; such as the day dawning upon a dark night, or the fountain of immortality issuing from chaos. She held in her hand a goblet of snow-cooled water, into which she dropped some sugar, and tempered it with spirit of wine; but I know not whether she scented it with attar, or sprinkled it with a few blossoms from her own rosy cheeks. In short, I received the beverage from her idol-fair hand; and, having drunk it off, found myself restored to a new life.

"Such is not my parching thirst that it is to be quenched
With the limpid element of water, were I to swallow it in oceans.

Joy to that happy aspect whose eye can every morning contemplate such a countenance as thine. A person intoxicated with wine lies giddy and awake half the night; but if intoxicated with the cupbearer (God), the day of judgment must be his dawn or morning."

XVI

In the year that Sultan Mohammed Khowarazm-Shah had for some political reason chosen to make peace with the King of Khota, I entered the metropolitan mosque at Kashghar, and met a youth incomparably lovely, and exquisitely handsome; such as they have mentioned in resemblance of him: "Thy master instructed thee in every bold and captivating grace; he taught thee coquetry and confidence, tyranny and violence." I have seen no mortal with such a form and temper, stateliness and manner; perhaps he learned these fascinating ways from an angel.

He held the introduction of the Zamakhshari Arabic grammar in his hand, and was repeating:—"Zaraba Zaidun Amranwa — Zaid beat Amru and is the assailant of Amru." I said: "O my son! the Khowarazm and Khatayi sovereigns have made peace, and does war thus subsist between Zaid and Amru?" He smiled, and asked me the place of my nativity. I answered: "The territory of Shiraz." He said: "Do you recollect any of Sadi's compositions?" I replied:

"I am enamored with the reader of the syntax,
Who, taking offense, assails me in like manner as Zaid does Amru.
And Zaid, when read Zaidin, can not raise his head;
And how canst thou give a *zammah* to a word accented with a *kasrah?*"

He reflected a little within himself, and said: "In these parts we have much of Sadi's compositions in the Persian language; if you will speak in that dialect we shall more readily comprehend you, for

"You should address mankind according to their capacities."

I replied: "Whilst thy passion was that of studying grammar, all trace of reason was erased from our hearts. Yes! the lover's heart is fallen a prey to thy snare: we are occupied about thee, and thou art taken up with Amru and Zaid."

On the morrow, which had been fixed on as the period of our stay, some of my fellow-travelers had perhaps told him such a one is Sadi; for I saw that he came running up, and expressed his affection and regret, saying: "Why did you not during all this time tell us that a certain person is Sadi, that I might have shown my gratitude by offering my service to your reverence?" I answered: "In thy presence I can not even say that I am I!"—He said: "How good it were if you would tarry here for a few days, that we might devote ourselves to your service." I replied: "That can not be, as this adventure will explain to you.—In the hilly region I saw a great and holy man, who was content in living retired from the world in a cavern. I said: 'Why dost thou not come into the city, that thy heart might be relieved from a load of servitude?' He replied: 'In it there dwell some wonderful and angel-faced charmers, and where the path is miry, elephants may find it slippery.'—Having delivered this speech, we kissed each other's head and face, and took our leaves.—What profits it to kiss our mistress's cheek, and with the same breath to bid her adieu? Thou mightest say that the apple had taken leave of its friends by having this cheek red and that cheek yellow:

"Were I not to die of grief on that day I say farewell,
Thou wouldst charge me with being insincere in my attachments."

XVII

A ragged dervish accompanied us along with the caravan for Hijaz, and a certain Arab prince presented him with a hundred dinars for the support of his family. Suddenly a gang of Khafachah robbers attacked the caravan, and completely stripped it. The merchants set up a weeping and wailing, and made much useless lamentation and complaint.—"Whether thou supplicatest them, or whether thou complainest, the robbers will not return thee their plunder": — all but that ragged wretch, who stood collected within himself, and unmoved by this adventure. I said: "Perhaps they did not plunder you of that money?" He replied: "Yes, they took it; but I was not so fond of my pet as to break my heart at parting with it. We should not fix our heart so on any thing or being as to find any difficulty in removing it."

I said: "What you have remarked corresponds precisely with what once befell myself; for in my juvenile days I took a liking to a young man, and so sincere was my attachment that the Kaaba, or fane, of my eye was his perfect beauty, and the profit of this life's traffic his much-coveted society.— Perhaps the angels might in paradise, otherwise no living form can on this earth display such a loveliness of person. By friendship I swear that after his demise all loving intercourse is forbidden; for no human emanation can stand a comparison with him.

"All at once the foot of his existence stumbled at the grave of annihilation; and the sigh of separation burst from the dwelling of his family. For many days I sat a fixture at his tomb, and, of the many dirges I composed upon his demise, this is one:

"'On that day, when thy foot was pierced with the thorn of death,
Would to God the hand of fate had cloven my head with the sword of destruction,
That my eyes might not this day have witnessed the world without thee.
Such am I, seated at the head of thy dust,
As the ashes are seated on my own:
Whoever could not take his rest and sleep
Till they first had spread a bed of roses and narcissuses for him:
The whirlwind of the sky has scattered the roses of his cheek,
And brambles and thorns are shooting from his grave.'

"After my separation from him I came to a steady and firm determination that during my remaining life I would fold up the carpet of enjoyment, and never re-enter the gay circle of society.— Were it not for the dread of its waves, much would be the profits of a voyage at sea; were it not for the vexation of the thorn, charming might be the society of the rose. Yesterday I was walking stately as a peacock in the garden of enjoyment; to-day I am writhing like a snake from the absence of my mistress."

XVIII

To a certain king of Arabia they were relating the story of Laila and Mujnun, and his insane state, saying: "Notwithstanding his knowledge and wisdom, he has turned his face toward the desert, and abandoned himself to distraction." The king ordered that they bring him into his presence; and he reproved him, and spoke, saying: "What have you seen unworthy in the noble nature of man that you should assume the manners of a brute, and forsake the enjoyment of human society?"

Mujnun wept and answered:

"Many of my friends reproach me for my love of her, namely
Laila.
Alas! that they could one day see her, that my excuse might be
manifest for me!

Would to God that such as blame me could behold thy face, O thou ravisher of hearts! that at the sight of thee they might, from inadvertency, cut their own fingers instead of the orange in their hands.— Then might the truth of the reality bear testimony against the semblance of fiction,

"What manner of person that was for whose sake you were
upbraiding me."

The king resolved within himself on viewing in person the charms of Laila, that he might be able to judge what her form could be which had caused all this misery, and ordered her to be produced in his presence. Having searched through the Arab tribes, they discovered and presented her before the king in the courtyard of his seraglio. He viewed her figure, and beheld a person of a tawny complexion and feeble frame of body. She appeared to him in a contemptible light, inasmuch as the lowest menial in his harem, or seraglio, surpassed her in beauty and excelled her in elegance. Mujnun, in his sagacity, penetrated what was passing in the royal mind, and said: "It would behoove you, O king, to contemplate the charms of Laila through the wicket of a Mujnun's eye, in order that the miracle of such a spectacle might be illustrated to you. Thou canst have no fellow-feeling for my disorder; a companion to suit me must have the self-same malady, that I may sit by him the livelong day repeating my tale; for by rubbing two pieces of dry firewood one upon another they will burn all the brighter:

"Had that grove of verdant reeds heard the murmurings of love
Which in detail of my mistress's story have passed through
my ear,
It would somehow have sympathized in my pain. Tell it, O
my friends, to such as are ignorant of love;
Would ye could be aware of what wrings me to the soul:

the anguish of a wound is not known to the hale and sound; we must detail our aches only to a fellow sufferer. It were idle to talk of a hornet to him who has never during his life smarted from its sting. Till thy condition may in some sort resemble mine, my state will seem to thee an idle fable. Compare not my pain with that of another man; he holds salt in his hand, but I hold it on a wounded limb."

XX

There was a handsome and well-disposed young man, who was embarked in a vessel with a lovely damsel. I have read that, sailing on the mighty deep, they fell together into a whirlpool. When the pilot came to offer him assistance, saying: "God forbid that he should perish in that distress," he was answering from the midst of that overwhelming vortex: "Leave me, and take the hand of my beloved!" The whole world admired him for this speech which, as he was expiring, he was heard to make. Learn not the tale of love from that faithless wretch who can neglect his beloved when exposed to danger. In this manner ended the lives of those lovers.

Listen to what has happened, that you may understand; for Sadi knows the ways and forms of courtship as well as the Tazi, or modern Arabic, is understood at Bagdad. Devote your whole heart to the heart-consoler you have chosen (namely, God), and let your eyes be shut to the whole world beside. Were Laila and Mujnun to return into life, they might read the history of love in this chapter.

Chapter VI

OF IMBECILITY AND OLD AGE

I

In the metropolitan mosque at Damascus I was engaged in a disputation with some learned men, when a youth suddenly entered the door, and said: "Does any of you understand the Persian language?" They directed him to me, and I answered: "It is true." He continued: "An old man of a hundred and fifty years of age is in the agonies of death, and is uttering something in the Persian language, which we do not understand. If you will have the goodness to go to him you may get rewarded; for he possibly may be dictating his will." When I sat down by his bedside I heard him reciting: "I said, I will enjoy myself for a few moments. Alas! that my soul took the path of departure. Alas! at the variegated table of life I partook of a few mouthfuls, and the fates said, enough!"

I explained the signification of these lines in Arabic to the Syrians. They were astonished that, at his advanced time of life, he should express himself so solicitous about a worldly existence. I asked him: "How do you now find yourself?" He replied: "What shall I say? — Hast thou never witnessed what torture that man suffers from whose jaw they are extracting a tooth? Fancy to thyself how excruciating is his pain from whose precious body they are tearing an existence!"

I said: "Banish all thoughts of death from your mind, and let not doubt undermine your constitution; for the Greek philosophers have remarked that although our temperaments are vigorous, that is no proof of a long life; and that although our sickness is dangerous, that is no positive sign of immediate dissolution. If you will give me leave, I will call in a physician to prescribe some medicine that may cure you." He replied: "Alas! alas! The landlord thinks of refreshing the paintings of his hall, and the house is tottering to its foundation. The physician smites the hands of despair when he sees the aged fallen in pieces like a potsherd; the old man bemoans himself in the agony of death while the old attendant nurse is anointing him with sandalwood. When the equipoise of the temperament is overset, neither amulets nor medicaments can do any good."

III

In the territory of Diarbekr, or Mesopotamia, I was the guest of an old man, who was very rich, and had a handsome son. One night he told a story, saying: "During my whole life I never had any child but this boy. And in this valley a certain tree is a place of pilgrimage, where people go to supplicate their wants; and many was the night that I have besought God at the foot of that tree before he would bestow upon me this boy." I have heard that the son was also whispering his companions, and saying: "How happy I should be if I could discover the site of that tree, in order that I might pray for the death of my father." The gentleman was rejoicing and saying: "What a sensible youth is my son!" and the boy was complaining and crying: "What a tedious old dotard is my father!" Many years are passing over thy head, during which thou didst not visit thy father's tomb. What pious oblation didst thou make to the manes of a parent that thou shouldst expect so much from thy son?

IV

Urged one day by the pride of youthful vanity, I had made a forced march, and in the evening found myself exhausted at the bottom of an acclivity. A feeble old man, who had deliberately followed the pace of the caravan, came up to me and said: "How come you to lie down here? Get up; this is no fit place to rest." I replied: "How can I proceed, who have not a foot to stand on?" He said: "Have you not heard what the prudent have remarked? 'Going on, and halting, is better than running ahead and breaking down!' Ye who wish to reach the end of your journey, hurry not on; practise my advice, and learn deliberation. The Arab horse makes a few stretches at full speed, and is broken down; while the camel, at its deliberate pace, travels on night and day, and gets to the end of his journey."

V

An active, merry, cheerful, and sweet-spoken youth was for a length of time in the circle of my society, whose heart had never known sorrow, nor his lip ceased from being on a smile. An age had passed, during which we had not chanced to meet. When I next saw him he had taken to himself a wife, and got a family; and the root of his enjoyment was torn up, and the rose of his mirth blasted. I asked him: "How is this?" He replied: "Since I became a father of children, I ceased to play the child.— Now thou art old, relinquish childishness, and leave it to the young to indulge in play and merriment. Expect not the sprightliness of youth from the aged; for the stream that ran by can never return. Now that the corn is ripe for the sickle, it rears not its head as when green and shooting. The season of youth has slipped through my hands; alas! when I think on those heart-exhilarating days! The lion has lost the sturdy grasp of his paw: I must now put up, like a lynx, with a bit of cheese. An old woman had stained her gray locks black. I said to her: O, my antiquated dame! thy hair I admit thou canst turn dark by art, but thou never canst make thy crooked back straight."

VI

One day, in the perverseness of youth, I spoke with asperity to my mother. Vexed at heart, she sat down in a corner, and with tears in her eyes was saying: "You have perhaps forgot the days of infancy, that you are speaking to me thus harshly.— How well did an old woman observe to her own son, when she saw him powerful as a tiger, and formidable as an elephant: 'Couldst thou call to mind those days of thy infancy when helpless thou wouldst cling to this my bosom, thou wouldst not thus assail me with savage fury, now thou art a lion-like hero, and I am a poor old woman.'"

VII

A rich miser had a son who was grievously sick. His well-wishers and friends spoke to him, saying: "It were proper that you either read the Koran throughout or offer an animal in sacrifice, in order that the Most High God may restore him to health." After a short reflection within himself he answered, "It is better to read the Koran, which is ready at hand; and my herds are at a distance." A good and holy man heard this and remarked: "He makes choice of the reading part because the Koran slips glibly over the tongue, but his money is to be wrung from the soul of him. Fie upon that readiness to bow the head in prayer; would that the hand of charity could accompany it! In bestowing a dinar he will stickle like an ass in the mire; but ask him to read the Al-hamdi, or first chapter of the Koran, and he will recite it a hundred times."

Chapter VII

OF THE IMPRESSIONS OF EDUCATION

I

A certain nobleman had a dunce of a son. He sent him to a learned man, saying: "Verily you will give instruction to this youth, peradventure he may become a rational being." He continued to give him lessons for some time, but they made no impression upon him, when he sent a message to the father, saying: "This son is not getting wise, and he has well-nigh made me a fool!" Where the innate capacity is good, education may make an impression upon it; but no furbisher knows how to give a polish to iron which is of a bad temper. Wash a dog seven times in the ocean, and so long as he is wet he is all the filthier. Were they to take the ass of Jesus to Mecca, on his return from that pilgrimage he would still be an ass.

II

A philosopher was exhorting his children and saying: "O emanations of my soul, acquire knowledge, as no reliance can be placed on worldly riches and possessions, for once you leave home rank is of no use, and gold and silver on a journey are exposed to the risk either of thieves plundering them at once, or of the owner wasting them by degrees; but knowledge is a perennial spring and ever-during fortune. Were a professional man to lose his fortune, he need not feel regret, for his knowledge is of itself a mine of wealth. Wherever he may sojourn the learned man will meet respect, and be ushered into the upper seat, whilst the ignorant man must put up with offal and suffer want.— If thou covet the paternal heritage, acquire thy father's knowledge, for this thy father's wealth thou may'st squander in ten days. After having been in authority, it is hard to obey; after having been fondled with caresses, to put up with men's violence.— There once occurred an insurrection in Syria, and everybody forsook his former peaceful abode. The sons of peasants, who were men of learning, came to be employed as the ministers of kings; and the children of noblemen, of bankrupt understandings, went a begging from village to village."

III

A certain learned man was superintending the education of a king's son; and he was chastising him without mercy, and reproving him with asperity. The boy, out of all patience, complained to the king his father, and laid bare before him his much-bruised body. The king was much offended, and sending for the master, said: "You do not treat the children of my meanest subject with the harshness and cruelty you do my boy; what do you mean by this?" He replied: "To think before they speak, and to deliberate before they act, are duties incumbent upon all mankind, and more immediately upon kings; because whatever may drop from their hands and tongue, the special deed or word will somehow become the subject of public animadversion; whereas any act or remark of the commonalty attracts not such notice.— Let a dervish, or poor man, commit a hundred indiscretions, and his companions will not notice one out of the hundred; and let a king but utter one foolish word, and it will be echoed from kingdom to kingdom: therefore in forming the morals of young princes, more pains are to be taken than with the sons of the vulgar. Whoever was not taught good manners in his boyhood, fortune will forsake him when he becomes a man. Thou may'st bend the green bough as thou likest; but let it once get dry, and it will require heat to straighten it:

"'Verily thou may'st bend the tender branch,
But it were labor lost to attempt making straight a crooked billet.'"

The king greatly approved of this ingenious detail, and the wholesome course of discipline of the learned doctor; and, bestowing upon him a dress and largess, raised him one step in his rank as a nobleman!

VI

A king gave his son into the charge of a preceptor, and said: "This is your child, educate him as you would one of your own." For some years he labored in teaching him, but to no good purpose; whilst the sons of the preceptor excelled in eloquence and knowledge. The king blamed the learned man, and remonstrated with him, saying: "You have violated your trust, and infringed the terms of your engagement." He replied: "O king, the education is the same, but their capacities are different!" Though silver and gold are extracted from stones, yet it is not in every stone that gold and silver are found. The Sohail, or star Canopus, is shedding his rays all over the globe. In one place he produces common leather, in another, or in Yamin, that called Adim, or perfumed.

VII

I heard a certain learned senior observing to a disciple: "If the sons of Adam were as solicitous after Providence, or God, as they are after their means of sustenance, their places in Paradise would surpass those of the angels." God did not overlook thee in that state when thou wert a senseless embryo in thy mother's womb. He bestowed upon thee a soul, reason, temper, intellect, symmetry, speech, judgment, understanding, and reflection. He accommodated thy hands with ten fingers, and suspended two arms from thy shoulders. Canst thou now suppose, O good-for-nothing wretch, that he will forget to provide thy daily bread?

VIII

I observed an Arab who was informing his son:

"O my child, God will ask thee on the day of judgment:
What hast thou done in this life?
But he will not inquire of thee:
Whence didst thou derive thy origin?"

That is, they (or God) will ask, saying: "What are your works?" But he will not question you, saying: "Who is your father?" The covering of the Kaaba at Mecca, which the pilgrims kiss from devotion, is not prized from its being the fabric of a silk-worm; for a while it associated with a venerable friend, and became, in consequence, venerable like him.

IX

They have related in the books of philosophers that scorpions are not brought forth according to the common course of nature, as other animals are, but that they eat their way through their mothers' wombs, tear open their bellies and thus make themselves a passage into the world; and that the fragments of skin which we find in scorpions' holes corroborate this fact. On one occasion I was stating this strange event to a good and great man, when he answered: "My heart is bearing testimony to the truth of this remark; nor can it be otherwise, for as they have thus behaved toward their parents in their youth, so they are approved and beloved in their riper years." On his death-bed a father exhorted his son, saying: "O generous youth, keep in mind this maxim: 'Whoever is ungrateful to his own kindred can not hope that fortune shall befriend him.'"

X

They asked a scorpion: "Why do you not make your appearance during the winter?" It answered: "What is my character in the summer that I should come abroad also in the winter?"

XIII

One year a dissension arose among the foot-travelers on a pilgrimage to Mecca, and the author (Sadi) was also a pedestrian among them. In truth, we fell head and ears together, and accusation and recrimination were bandied from all sides. I overheard a *kajawah,* or gentleman, riding on one side of a camel-litter, observing to his *adil,* or opposite companion: "How strange that the ivory *piyadah,* or pawns, on reaching the top of the *shatranj,* or chess-board, become *fazzin,* or queens; that is, they get rank, or become better than they were; and the *piyadah,* or pawns, of the pilgrimage — that is, our foot-pilgrims — have crossed the desert and become worse." Say from me to that *haji,* or pilgrim, the pest of his fellow-pilgrims, that he lacerates the skin of mankind by his contention. Thou art not a real pilgrim, but that meek camel is one who is feeding on thorns and patient under its burden.

XIV

A Hindu, or Indian, was teaching the art of playing off fireworks. A philosopher observed to him: "This is an unfit sport for you, whose dwelling is made of straw." Utter not a word till thou knowest that it is the mirror of what is correct; and do not put a question where thou knowest that the answer must be unfavorable.

XV

A fellow had a complaint in his eyes, and went to a horse-doctor, saying: "Prescribe something for me." The doctor of horses applied to his eyes what he was in the habit of applying to the eyes of quadrupeds, and the man became blind. They carried their complaint before the *hakim,* or judge. He decreed: "This man has no redress, for had he not been an ass he would not have applied to a horse or ass doctor!" The moral of this apologue is, that whoever doth employ an inexperienced person on an affair of importance, besides being brought to shame, he will incur from the wise the imputation of a weak mind. A prudent man, with an enlightened understanding, entrusts not affairs of consequence to one of mean capacity. The plaiter of mats, notwithstanding he be a weaver, they would not employ in a silk manufactory.

XVI

A certain great Imaan had a worthy son, and he died. They asked him, saying: "What shall we inscribe upon the urn at his tomb?" He replied: "Verses of the holy Koran are of such superior reverence and dignity that they should not be written in places where time might efface, mankind tread upon, or dogs defile them; yet, if an epitaph be necessary, let these two couplets suffice: I said:

"'Alas! how grateful it was proving to my heart,
So long as the verdure of thy existence might flourish in the garden.'

He replied: 'O my friend, have patience till the return of the spring, and thou may'st again see roses blossoming on my bosom, or shooting from my dust.'"

XVII

A holy man was passing by a wealthy personage's mansion, and saw him with a slave tied up by the hands and feet, and giving him chastisement. He said: "O my son! God Almighty has made a creature like yourself subject to your command, and has given you a superiority over him. Render thanksgiving to the Most High Judge, and deal not with him so savagely; lest hereafter, on the day of judgment, he may prove the more worthy of the two, and you be put to shame.— Be not so enraged with thy bondsman; torture not his body, nor harrow up his heart. Thou mightest buy him for ten dinars, but hadst not after all the power of creating him.— To what length will this authority, pride, and insolence hurry thee; there is a Master mightier than thou art. Yes, thou art a lord of slaves and vassals, but do not forget thine own Lord Paramount — namely, God!" There is a tradition of the prophet Mohammed, on whom be blessing, announcing: On the day of resurrection, that will be the most mortifying event when the good slave will be taken up to heaven, and the wicked master sent down to hell.—" Upon the bondsman, who is subservient to thy command, wreak not thy rage and boundless displeasure. For it must be disgraceful on the day of reckoning to find the slave at liberty and the master in bondage."

Chapter VIII

OF THE DUTIES OF SOCIETY

I

Riches are intended for the comfort of life, and not life for the purpose of hoarding riches. I asked a wise man, saying: "Who is the fortunate man, and who is the unfortunate?" He said: "That man was fortunate who spent and gave away, and that man unfortunate who died and left behind.— Pray not for that good-for-nothing man who did nothing, for he passed his life in hoarding riches, and did not spend them."

II

The prophet Moses, on whom be peace, admonished Carum, saying: "Be bounteous in like manner as God has been bounteous to thee": but he listened not, and you have heard the end of him. Whoever did not an act of charity with his silver and gold sacrificed his future prospects on his hoard of gold and silver. If desirous that thou shouldst benefit by the wealth of this world, be generous with thy fellow creature, as God has been generous with thee.

The Arabs say:

> "Show thy generosity, but make it not obligatory,
> That the benefit of it may redound to thee":

that is, bestow and make presents, but do not exact an obligation that the profit of that act may be returned to you. Wherever the tree of generosity strikes root it sends forth its boughs, and they shoot above the skies. If thou cherishest a hope of enjoying its fruit, by gratitude I entreat of thee not to lay a saw upon its trunk. Render thanks to God, that thou wert found worthy of his divine grace, that he has not excluded thee from the riches of his bounty. Esteem it no obligation that thou art serving the king, but show thy gratitude to him, namely God, who has placed thee in this service.

III

Two person labored to a vain, and studied to an unprofitable end: he who hoarded wealth and did not spend it, and he who acquired science and did not practise it. — However much thou art read in theory, if thou hast no practise thou art ignorant. He is neither a sage philosopher nor an acute divine, but a beast of burden with a load of books. How can that brainless head know or comprehend whether he carries on his back a library or bundle of fagots?

IV

Learning is intended to fortify religious practise, and not to gratify worldly traffic.— Whoever prostituted his temperance, piety, and science, gathered his harvest into a heap and set fire to it.

V

An intemperate man of learning is like a blind link-boy:

> He shows the road to others, but sees it not himself:

Whoever ventured his life on an unproductive hazard gained nothing by the risk, and lost his own stake.

VI

A kingdom is embellished by the wise, and religion rendered illustrious by the pious. Kings stand more in need of the company of the intelligent than the intelligent do of the society of kings.— If, O king! thou wilt listen to my advice, in all thy archives thou canst not find a wiser maxim than this: entrust thy concerns only to the learned, notwithstanding business is not a learned man's concern.

VII

Three things have no durability without their concomitants: property without trade, knowledge without debate, or a sovereignty without government.

VIII

To compassionate the wicked is to tyrannize over the good; and to pardon the oppressor is to deal harshly with the oppressed.— When thou patronizest and succorest the base-born man, he looks to be made the partner of thy fortune.

IX

No reliance can be placed on the friendship of kings, nor vain hope put in the melodious voice of boys; for that passes away like a vision, and this vanishes like a dream.— Bestow not thy affections upon a mistress who has a thousand lovers; or, if thou bestowest them upon her, be prepared for a separation.

X

Reveal not every secret you have to a friend, for how can you tell but that friend may hereafter become an enemy? And bring not all the mischief you are able to do upon an enemy, for he may one day become your friend. And any private affair that you wish to keep secret, do not divulge to anybody; for, though such a person has your confidence, none can be so true to your secret as yourself.— Silence is safer than to communicate the thought of thy mind to anybody, and to warn him, saying: Do not divulge it, O silly man! confine the water at the dam-head, for once it has a vent thou canst not stop it. Thou shouldst not utter a word in secret which thou wouldst not have spoken in the face of the public.

XI

A reduced foe, who offers his submission and courts your amity, can only have in view to become a strong enemy, as they have said: "You can not trust the sincerity of friends, then what are you to expect from the cajoling of foes?" Whoever despises a weak enemy resembles him who neglects a spark of fire.— To-day that thou canst quench it, put it out; for let fire rise into a flame, and it may consume a whole world. Now that thou canst transfix him with thy arrow, permit not thy antagonist to string his bow.

XIII

Whoever is making a league with their enemies has it in his mind to do his friends an ill turn.—"O wise man! wash thy hands of that friend who is in confederacy with thy foes."

XIV

When irresolute in the dispatch of business, incline to that side which is the least offensive.— Answer not with harshness a mild-spoken man, nor force him into war who knocks at the gate of peace.

XV

So long as money can answer, it were wrong in any business to put the life in danger — as the Arabs say:

"Let the sword decide after stratagem has failed":

When the hand is balked in every crafty endeavor, it is lawful to lay it upon the hilt of the saber.

XVI

Show no mercy to a subdued foe, for if he recover himself he will show you no mercy.— When thou seest thy antagonist in a reduced state, curl not thy whiskers at him in contempt, for in every bone there is marrow, and within every jacket there is a man.

XVII

Whoever puts a wicked man to death delivers mankind from his mischief, and the wretch himself from God's vengeance.— Beneficence is praiseworthy; yet thou shouldst not administer a balsam to the wound of the wicked. Knew he not who took compassion on a snake, that it is the pest of the sons of Adam.

XVIII

It is wrong to follow the advice of an adversary; nevertheless it is right to hear it, that you may do the contrary; and this is the essence of good policy.— Sedulously shun whatever thy foe may recommend, otherwise thou may'st wring the hands of repentance on thy knees. Should he show thee to the right a path straight as an arrow, turn aside from that, and take the path to the left.

XX

Two orders of mankind are the enemies of church and State: the king without clemency, and the holy man without learning.— Let not that prince have rule over the State who is not himself obedient to the will of God.

XXI

It behooves a king so to regulate his anger toward his enemies as not to alarm the confidence of his friends; for the fire of passion falls first on the angry man; afterward its sparks will dart forth toward the foe, and him they may reach, or they may not. It ill becomes the children of Adam, formed of dust, to harbor in their heads such pride, arrogance, and passion. I can not fancy all this thy warmth and obstinacy to be created from earth, but from fire. I went to a holy man in the land of Bailcan, and said: "Cleanse me of ignorance by thy instruction!" He replied: "O *fakih,* or theologician! go and bear things patiently like the earth;

or whatever thou hast read let it all be buried under the earth."

XXII

An evil-disposed man is a captive in the hands of an enemy (namely, himself); for wherever he may go he can not escape from the grasp of that enemy's vengeance.— Let a wicked man ascend up to heaven, that he may escape from the grasp of calamity; even thither would the hand of his own evil heart follow him with misfortune.

XXIII

When you see discord raging among the troops of your enemy, be on your side quiet; but if you see them united, think of your own dispersed state.— When thou beholdest war among thy foes, go and enjoy peace with thy friends; but if thou findest them of one soul and mind, string thy bow, and range stones around thy battlements.

XXVIII

Whoever is counseling a self-sufficient man stands himself in need of a counselor.

XXIX

Swallow not the wheedling of a rival, nor pay for the sycophancy of a parasite; for that has laid the snare of treachery, and this whetted the palate of gluttony. The fool is puffed up with his own praise, like a dead body, which on being stretched upon a bier shows a momentary corpulency. — Take heed and listen not to the sycophant's blandishments, who expects in return some small compensation; for shouldst thou any day disappoint his object he would in like style sum up two hundred of thy defects.

XXX

Till some person may show its defects, the speech of the orator will fail of correctness.— Be not vain of the eloquence of thy discourse because it has the fool's good opinion, and thine own approbation.

XXXI

Every person thinks his own intellect perfect, and his own child handsome.— A Mussulman and a Jew were warm in argument to such a degree that I smiled at their subject. The Mussulman said in wrath: "If this deed of conveyance be not authentic may I, O God, die a Jew!" The Jew replied: "On the Pentateuch I swear, if what I say be false, I am a Mussulman like you!" Were intellect to be annihilated from the face of the earth, nobody could be brought to say: "I am ignorant."

XXXII

Ten people will partake of the same joint of meat, and two dogs will snarl over a whole carcass. The greedy man is incontinent with a whole world set before him; the temperate man is content with his crust of bread.— A loaf of brown bread may fill an empty stomach, but the produce of the whole globe can not satisfy a greedy eye.— My father, when the sun of his life was going down, gave me this sage advice, and it set for good, saying: "Lust is a fire; refrain from indulging it, and do not involve thyself in the flames of hell. Since thou hast not the strength of burning in those flames (as a punishment in the next world), pour in this world the water of continence upon this fire — namely, lust."

XXXIII

Whoever does not do good, when he has the means of doing it, will suffer hardship when he has not the means.— None is more unlucky than the misanthrope, for on the day of adversity he has not a single friend.

XXXIV

Life stands on the verge of a single breath; and this world is an existence between two nonentities. Such as truck their *deen,* or religious practise, for worldly pelf are asses. They sold Joseph, and what got they by their bargain? — "Did I not covenant with you, O ye sons of Adam, that you should not serve Satan; for verily he is your avowed enemy."— By the advice of a foe you broke your faith with a friend; behold from whom you separated, and with whom you united yourselves.

XXXVI

Whatever is produced in haste goes hastily to waste.— I have heard that, after a process of forty years, they convert the clay of the East into a China porcelain cup. At Bagdad they can make a hundred cups in a day, and thou mayst of course conceive their respective value. A chicken walks forth from its shell, and goes in quest of its food; the young of man possesses not that instinct of prudence and discrimination. That which was at once something comes to nothing; and this surpasses all creatures in dignity and wisdom. A piece of crystal or glass is found everywhere, and held of no value; a ruby is obtained with difficulty, and therefore inestimable.

XXXVII

Patience accomplishes its object, while hurry speeds to its ruin.— With my own eyes I saw in the desert that the deliberate man outstripped him that had hurried on. The wing-footed steed is broken down in his speed, whilst the camel-driver jogs on with his beast to the end of his journey.

XXXVIII

Nothing is so good for an ignorant man as silence, and if he knew this he would no longer be ignorant.— When unadorned with the grace of eloquence it is wise to keep watch over the tongue in the mouth. The tongue, by abuse, renders a man contemptible; levity in a nut is a sign of its being empty. A fool was undertaking the instruction of an ass, and had devoted his whole time to this occupation. A wise man said to him: "What art thou endeavoring to do? In this vain attempt dread the reproof of the censorious! A brute can never learn speech from thee; do thou learn silence from him." That man who reflects not before he speaks will only make all the more improper answer. Either like a man arrange thy speech with judgment, or like a brute sit silent.

XXXIX

Whoever shall argue with one more learned than himself that others may take him for a wise man, only confirms them in his being a fool.—"When a person superior to what thou art engages thee in conversation do not contradict him, though thou mayst know better."

XL

He can see no good who will associate with the wicked.—Were an angel from heaven to associate with a demon, he would learn his brutality, perfidy, and hypocrisy. Virtue thou never canst learn of the vicious; it is not the wolf's occupation to mend skins, but to tear them.

XLI

Expose not the secret failings of mankind, otherwise you must verily bring scandal upon them and distrust upon yourself.

XLII

Whoever acquires knowledge and does not practise it resembles him who plows his land and leaves it unsown.

XLVI

It is not every man that has a handsome physical exterior that has a good moral character; for the faculty of business or virtue resides in the heart and not in the skin. Thou canst in one day ascertain the intellectual faculties of a man, and what proficiency he has made in his degrees of knowledge; but be not secure of his mind, nor foolishly sure, for it may take years to detect the innate baseness of the heart.

XLVII

Whoever contends with the great sheds his own blood.—Thou contemplatest thyself as a mighty great man; and they have truly remarked that the squinter sees double. Thou, who canst in play butt with a ram, must soon find thyself with a broken pate.

XLVIII

To grapple with a lion, or to box against a naked scimitar, are not the acts of the prudent.— Brave not the furious with war and opposition; before their arms of strength cross thy hands of submission.

XLIX

A weak man, who tries his courage against the strong, leagues with the foe to his own destruction.— Nurtured in a shade, what strength can he have that he should engage with the warlike in battle; impotent of arm, he was falling the victim of folly when he set his wrist in opposition to a wrist of iron.

L

Whoever will not listen to admonition harbors the fancy of hearing reprehension.— When advice gains not an admission into the ear, if I give thee reproof, hear it in silence.

LI

The idle can not endure the industrious any more than the curs of the market-place, who, on meeting dogs employed for sporting, will snarl at and prevent them passing.

LII

A mean wretch, that can not vie with another in virtue, will assail him with malignity.— The narrow-minded envier will somehow manage to revile thee, who in thy presence might have the tongue of his utterance struck dumb.

LV

To hold counsel with women is bad, and to deal generously with prodigals a fault.— Showing mercy upon the sharp-fanged pard must prove an injustice to the harmless sheep.

LVI

Whoever has his foe at his mercy, and does not kill him, is his own enemy.— With a stone in his hand, and the snake's head convenient, a wise man hesitates not in crushing it.

Certain people have seen this maxim in an opposite point of view, saying: "It were wiser to delay the execution of captives, inasmuch as the option is left so that you can slay, or you can release them; but if you shall have heedlessly put them to death, the policy is defunct, for the opportunity of repairing is lost."— There is no great difficulty to separate the soul from the body, but it is not so easy to restore life to the dead: prudence dictates patience in giving the arrow flight, for let it quit the bow and it never can be recalled.

LVII

A learned man who has got into an argument with the ignorant can have no hopes of supporting his own dignity; and if an ignoramus by his loquacity gets the upper hand it should not surprise us, for he is a stone and can bruise a gem.— No wonder if his spirit flag; the nightingale is cooped up in the same cage with the crow.— If the man of sense is coarsely treated by the vulgar, let it not excite our wrath and indignation; if a piece of worthless stone can bruise a cup of gold, its worth is not increased, nor that of the gold diminished.

LX

Genius without education is the subject of our regret, and education without genius is labor lost. Although embers have a lofty origin (fire being of a noble nature), yet, as having no intrinsic worth, they fall upon a level with common dust; on the other hand, sugar does not derive its value from the cane, but from its own innate quality.— Inasmuch as the disposition of Canaan was bad, his descent from the prophet Noah stood him in no stead. Pride thyself on what virtue thou hast, and not on thy parentage; the rose springs from a thorn-bush, and Abraham from Azor (either his father's name, or fire).

LXI

That is musk which discloses itself by its smell, and not what the perfumers impose upon us.—If a man be expert in any art he needs not tell it, for his own skill will show it.

LXII

A wise man is like a vase in a druggist's shop, silent, but full of virtues; and the ignorant man resembles the drum of the warrior, being full of noise, and an empty babbler.— The sincerely devout have remarked that a learned man, beset by the illiterate, is like one of the lovely in a circle of the blind, or the holy Koran in the dwelling of the infidel.

LXIII

A friend whom they take an age to conciliate, it were wrong all at once to alienate.— In a series of years a stone changes into a ruby; take heed, and destroy it not at once by dashing it against another stone.

LXIV

Reason is in like manner enthralled by passion, as an uxorious man is in the hands of an artful woman. Thou mayst shut the door of joy upon that dwelling where thou hearest resounding the scolding voice of a woman.

LXV

Intellect, without firmness, is craft and chicanery; and firmness, without intellect, perverseness and obstinacy.— First, prudence, good sense, and discrimination, and then dominion; for the dominion and good fortune of the ignorant are the armor of rebellion against God.

LXVI

The sinner who spends and gives away is better than the devotee who begs and lays by.

LXVII

Whoever foregoes carnal indulgence in order to get the good opinion of mankind, has forsaken a lawful passion and involved himself in what is forbidden.— What, wretched creature! can that hermit see in his own tarnished mirror, or heart, who retires to a cell, but not for the sake of God?

LXIX

A wise man should not through clemency overlook the

insolence of the vulgar, otherwise both sustain a loss, for their respect for him is lessened and their own brutality confirmed: — When thou addressest the low with urbanity and kindness, it only adds to their pride and arrogance.

LXXIV

In a season of drought and scarcity ask not the distressed dervish, saying: "How are you?" Unless on the condition that you apply a balm to his wound, and supply him with the means of subsistence.— The ass which thou seest stuck in the slough with his rider, compassionate from thy heart, otherwise do not go near him. Now that thou went and asked him how he fell, like a sturdy fellow bind up thy loins, and take his ass by the tail.

LXXV

Two things are repugnant to reason: to expend more than what Providence has allotted for us, and to die before our ordained time.— Whether offered up in gratitude, or uttered in complaint, destiny can not be altered by a thousand sighs and lamentations. The angel who presides over the storehouse of the winds feels no compunction, though he extinguish the old woman's lamp.

LXXVI

O you that are going in quest of food, sit down, that you may have to eat. And, O you that death is in quest of, go not on, for you can not carry life along with you.— In search of thy daily bread, whether thou exertest thyself, or whether thou dost not, the God of Majesty and Glory will equally provide it. Wert thou to walk into the mouth of a tiger or lion, he could not devour thee, unless by the ordinance of thy destiny.

LXXVII

Whatever was not designed, the hand can not reach; and whatever was ordained, it can attain in any situation.— Thou hast heard that Alexander got as far as chaos; but after all this toil he drank not the water of immortality.

CROSSING THE PERSIAN DESERT.

LXXVIII

The fisherman, unless it be his lot, catches no fish in the Tigris; and the fish, unless it be its fate, does not die on the dry land.— The wretched miser is prowling all over the world, he in quest of pelf, and death in quest of him.

LXXXI

The envious man is niggard of the gifts of Providence, and an enemy of the innocent.— I met a dry-brained fellow of this sort, tricked forth in the robe of a dignified person. I said: "O sir! if thou art unfortunate in having this disposition, in what have the fortunate been to blame? — Take heed, and wish not misfortune to the misanthrope, for his own ill-conditioned lot is calamity sufficient. What need is there of showing ill-will to him, who has such an enemy close at his heels?"

LXXXII

A scholar without diligence is a lover without money; a traveler without knowledge is a bird without wings; a theorist without practise is a tree without fruit; and a devotee without learning is a house without an entrance.

LXXXIII

The object of sending the Koran down from heaven was that mankind might make it a manual of morals, and not that they should recite it by sections.

LXXXIV

The sincere publican has proceeded on foot; the slothful Pharisee is mounted and gone asleep.

LXXXV

The sinner who humbles himself in prayer is more acceptable than the devotee who is puffed up with pride.— The courteous and kind-hearted soldier of fortune is better than the misanthropic and learned divine.

LXXXVI

A learned man without works is a bee without honey.— Tell that harsh and ungenerous hornet: As thou yieldest no honey, wound not with thy sting.

LXXXIX

Though a dress presented by the sovereign be honorable, yet is our own tattered garment preferable; and though the viands at a great man's table be delicate, yet is our own homely fare more sweet.— A salad and vinegar, the produce of our own industry, are sweeter than the lamb and bread sauce at the table of our village chief.

XC

It is contrary to sound judgment, and repugnant to the maxims of the prudent, to take a medicine on conjecture, or to follow a road but in the track of a caravan.

XCI

They asked Imaam Mursheed Mohammed-bin-Mohammed Ghazali, on whom be God's mercy, how he had reached such a pitch of knowledge. He replied: "Whatever I was ignorant of myself, I felt no shame in asking of others."— Thy prospect of health conforms with reason, when thy pulse is in charge of a skilled physician. Ask whatever thou knowest not; for the condescension of inquiring is a guide on thy road in the excellence of learning.

XCII

Anything you foresee that you may somehow come to know, be not hasty in questioning, lest your consequence and respectability may suffer.— When Lokman perceived that in the hands of David iron was miraculously molded like wax, he asked him not, How didst thou do it? for he was aware that he should know it, through his own wisdom, without asking.

XCIII

It is one of the laws of good breeding that you should forego an engagement or accommodate yourself to the master of the entertainment.— If thou knowest that the inclination is reciprocal, accommodate thy story to the temper of the hearer. Any discreet man that was in Mujnun's company would entertain him only with encomiums on Laila.

XCVIII

To tell a falsehood is like the cut of a saber; for though the wound may heal, the scar of it will remain. In like manner as the brothers of the blessed Joseph, who, being notorious for a lie, had no credit afterward when they spoke the truth: God on high has said — Jacob is supposed to speak — (Koran xii. Sale ii. 35): "Nay, but rather ye have contrived this to gratify your own passion; yet it behooves me to be patient."— If a man who is in the habit of speaking truth lets a mistake escape him, we can overlook it; but if he be notorious for uttering falsehoods, and tell a truth, thou wilt call it a lie.

XCIX

The noblest of creatures is man, and the vilest of animals is no doubt a dog; yet, in the concurring opinion of the wise, a dog, thankful for his food, is more worthy than a human being who is void of gratitude.— A dog will never forget the crumb thou gavest him, though thou mayst afterward throw a hundred stones at his head; but foster with thy kindness a low man for an age, and on the smallest provocation he will be up against thee in arms.

CI

It is written in the Injeel, or Gospel, stating: "O son of man, if I bestow riches upon you you will be more intent upon your property than upon me, and if I leave you in poverty you will sit down dejected; how then can you feel a relish to praise, or a zeal to worship me?" (Proverbs xxx. 7, 8, 9).— In the day of plenty thou art proud and negligent; in the time of want, full of sorrow and dejected; since in prosperity and adversity such is thy condition, it were difficult to state when thou wouldst voluntarily do thy duty.

CII

The pleasure of Him, or God, who has no equal, hurls one man from a throne of sovereignty, and another he preserves in a fish's belly.— Happy proceeds his time who is enraptured with thy praise, though, like Jonah, he even may pass it in the belly of a fish!

CIII

Were the Almighty to unsheath the sword of his wrath, prophets and patriarchs would draw in their heads; and were he to deign a glimpse of his benevolence, it would reach the wicked along with the good.— Were he on the day of judgment to call us to a strict account, even the prophets would have no room for excuse. Say, withdraw the veil from the face of thy compassion, that sinners may entertain hopes of pardon.

CIV

Whoever is not to be brought into the path of righteousness by the punishments of this life shall be overtaken with the punishments of that to come: "Verily, I will cause them to taste the lesser punishment over and above the greater punishment" (Koran xxxii. Sale ii. 258).— Princes, in chastising, admonish, and then confine; when they admonish, and thou listenest not, they throw thee into prison.

CV

Men of auspicious fortune would rather take warning from the precepts and examples of their predecessors than that the rising generation should take warning from their acts.— The bird will not approach the grain that is spread about, where it sees another bird a captive in the snare. Take warning by the mischance of others, that others may not take warning by thine.

CVI

How can he help himself who was born deaf, if he can not

hear; and what can he do whose thread of fortune is dragging him on that he may not proceed?— The dark night of such as are beloved of God is serene and light as the bright day; but this good fortune results not from thine own strength of arm, till God in his mercy deign to bestow it. To whom shall I complain of thee? for there is no judge else, nor is any arm mightier than thine. Him whom thou directest none can lead astray, and him whom thou bewilderest none can direct upon his way.

CVII

The beggar whose end is good is better off than the king whose end is evil.— That sorrow which is the harbinger of joy is preferable to the joy which is followed by sorrow.

CVIII

The sky enriches the earth with rain, and the earth gives it dust in return. As the Arabs say: "What the vessels have, that they give."— If my moral character strike thee as improper, do not renounce thine own good character.

CIX

The Most High God discerns and hides what is improper; my neighbor sees not, and is loud in his clamor.— God preserve us! if man knew what is hidden, none could be safe from the animadversion of his neighbor.

CX

Gold is got from the mine by digging into the earth; and from the grasp of the miser by taking away his life.— Misers spend not, but watch with solicitude: expectation, they say, is preferable to waste. Next day observe to the joy of their enemies, the gold remains, and they are dead without the enjoyment of that hope.

CXI

Such as deal hard with the weak will suffer from the extortion of the strong.— It is not every arm in which there is strength that can wrench the hand of a weak man. Bring not affliction upon the hearts of the feeble, lest thou mayst fall under the lash of the strong.

CXII

A wise man, where he meets opposition, labors to get through it, and where he finds quiet he drops his anchor, for there safety is on one side, and here enjoyment in the middle of it.

CXIII

The gamester wants three sixes, but he throws only three aces.— The pasture meadow is a thousand times richer than the common, but the horse has not his tether at command.

CXIV

The dervish in his prayer is saying: "O God, have compassion on the wicked, for to the good thou hast been abundantly kind, inasmuch as thou hast made them virtuous."

CXV

Jemshid was the first person who put an edging round his garment, and a ring upon his finger. They asked him: "Why did you bestow all the decoration and ornament on the left hand, whilst the right is the superior?" He answered: "Sufficient for the right is the ornament of being right." Feridun commanded the gilders of China that they would inscribe upon the front of his palace: "Strive, O wise man, to make the wicked good, for the good are of themselves great and fortunate."

CXVI

They said to a great and holy man: "Notwithstanding the superiority that the right hand commands, why do they wear the ring on the left hand?" He replied: "Are you not aware that the best are most neglected!" He who casts our horoscope, provision, and fortune, bestows upon us either good luck or wisdom."

CXVII

It is proper for him to offer counsel to kings who dreads not to lose his head, nor looks for a reward.— Whether thou strewest heaps of gold at his feet, or brandishest an Indian sword over the Unitarian's head, to hope or fear he is alike indifferent; and in this the divine unity alone he is resolved and firm.

CXVIII

It belongs to the king to displace extortioners, to the superintendent of the police to guard against murderers, and to the cazi to decide in quarrels and disputes. No two complainants ever referred to the cazi content to abide by justice. When thou knowest that in right the claim is just, better pay with a grace than by distress and force. If a man is refractory in discharging his revenue, the collector must necessarily coerce him to pay it.

CXIX

Every man's teeth are blunted by acids excepting the cazi's, and they require sweets.— That cazi, or judge, that can accept of five cucumbers as a bribe will confirm thee in a right to ten fields of melons.

CXXI

They asked a wise man, saying: "Of the many celebrated trees which the Most High God has created lofty and umbrageous, they call none *azad,* or free, excepting the cypress, which bears no fruit; what mystery is there in this?" He replied: "Each has its appropriate produce and appointed season, during the continuance of which it is fresh and blooming, and during their absence dry and withered; to neither of which states is the cypress exposed, being always flourishing; and of this nature are the *azads,* or religious independents. Fix not thy heart on what is transitory; for the Dijlah, or Tigris, will continue to flow through Bagdad after the race of Califs is extinct. If thy hand has plenty, be liberal as the date-tree; but if it affords nothing to give away, be an *azad,* or free man, like the cypress.

CXXII

Two orders of mankind died, and carried with them regret: such as had and did not spend, and such as knew and did not practise.— None can see that wretched mortal a miser who will not endeavor to point out his faults; but were the generous man to have a hundred defects, his liberality would cover all his blemishes.

Colophon

The book of the "Gulistan, or Flower-Garden," was completed through the assistance and grace of God. Throughout the whole of this work I have not followed the custom of writers by inserting verses of poetry borrowed from former authors: "It is more decorous to wear our own patched and old cloak than to ask in loan another man's garment."

Most of these sayings have a dash of hilarity and an odor of gaiety about them, in consequence of which short-sighted critics extend the tongue of animadversion, saying: "It is not the occupation of sensible men to solicit marrow from a shriveled brain, or to digest the smoke of a profitless lamp." Nevertheless it can not be concealed from the enlightened judgment of the holy and good, to whom these discourses are specially addressed, that the pearls of salutary admonition are threaded on the cord of an elegance of language, and the bitter potion of instruction sweetened with the honey of facetiousness, that the taste of the reader may not take disgust, and himself be debarred from the pleasure of approving of them: "On our part we offered some good advice, and spent an age in bringing it to perfection. If that should not meet the ear of anybody's good-will, prophets deliver their messages, or warn mankind; and that is enough."

O thou who perusest this book, ask the mercy of God on the author of it: his forgiveness on the transcriber. Petition for whatever charitable gift thou mayst require for thyself, and implore pardon on the owner. The book is finished through the favor of the Lord God Paramount and the bestower of all good!

Printed in the United States
116873LV00004B/93/A

9 781425 328009